SMALL TALK

Relationship building and the art of persuasion. How to Confide in People, Calm Your Nerves, and Boost Your Charm (2022 Guide for Beginners)

Christopher Cannon

Contents

INTRODUCTION

Congratulations and thank you for downloading Small Talk. Being social can be difficult at times, especially when attempting to interact with new people. This is because you may be lacking in favorable topics, to begin with, as well as dealing with other related issues such as anxiety. As a result, this is the book you've been looking for to help you make small talk and improve your social skills.

The chapters that follow will go over important guidelines to help you with various aspects of developing your social interactions. With some having a problem because of their state of mind, it is critical to understand how to approach someone even if you have had limited interactions in the past. As a result, you will learn how to manage your mindset when you have certain beliefs, thoughts, and imaginations about how you should interact with others. As a result, you will learn how to control your thoughts. That is, you will discover that others do not perceive you in the way you perceive them.

There are also times when you have a great attitude when it comes to making small talk with others but are experiencing some negative emotions within yourself. These may include social anxiety, particularly when making your first impression in a conversation. As a result, this book will assist you in understanding how to control and manage these emotions, as well as how to carry yourself during the first impression in a conversation. Aside from that, you'll learn the general rules of small talk, which will help you have great conversations with others.

There are many books on this subject available, so thank you for selecting this one! Every effort has been made to include as much useful information as possible; please enjoy!

CHAPTER 1

How to Develop a Positive Attitude and the Basics of Small Talk

Meeting new people and starting a formal conversation may seem strange and unnecessary at times unless you are meeting for official purposes. When developing a topic of conversation with new people, however, it is critical, to begin with, small talk, which builds up a conversation. There are numerous topics from which to choose, and then develop a meaningful discussion from other relevant topics. Small talks are defined as informal conversations or dialogues that do not always cover the functional or transactional topic. As a result, it is referred to as a social skill because it allows people to freely communicate with others, including strangers.

The small talk became a phenomenon in 1923 when Bronislaw Malinowski studied it and described it as a social skill and a type of social communication. Small discussions can also be used as space fillers to avoid silence during conversations, in addition to acting as a type of conversation opener. Others use small talk to limit rejections associated with the end of a particular topic. Some discussions have limited topics to cover; as a result, small talk is required to promote conversations between different people, including family members, friends, co-workers, and new people. According to researchers, the nature of the relationship between the two parties involved in the conversation may be the most important factor in small talk.

Small talk patterns have been linked to chances when meeting strangers and establishing topics that are typically agreed upon by the other person. It could be a question, an opinion, or a statement that requires a response. When considering politeness, the person responds with a short and substantial answer. In this case, you can either engage further in the topic or change the subject immediately after consideration for the following topic small talks are typically brief and serve as tools for maintaining a conversation in the absence of a meaningful discussion. A study suggests that because women are more collaborative among themselves, they can engage in different small talks more frequently than men due to their involvement in conversations.

SMALL TALK TOPICS FOR A MORE FRIENDLY CONVERSATION

Introducing Yourself

Meeting new people, particularly those you admire can be accomplished through the use of small talk, which promotes the development of a significant conversation. That is, you can approach and introduce yourself to someone with whom you have never previously interacted. You can include some details about how you first saw the individual or what you do during the introduction. "Hello Angel, we always have coffee at the same place and time, but we've never spoken." "My name is [Your name]."

General Subjects

There are several small talk topics from which to choose and engage to develop a conversation. You can discuss the weather, sports, or recent news stories that have made headlines.

Such universal topics are important, especially for groups, because some people may be unaware of the topic, but one or more may be. Some people may not be sports or news fans, but you can try to make it more general to appeal to their interests. Don't get too deep into topics, making others feel excluded, but make it more interactive.

Discuss the Day

This is one of the small talks you can use when you don't know where to begin or how to break the silence. When it comes to depending on which option you select, the day could be about your day or their day. Even those who are having a bad day can start a conversation by making it more positive. However, avoid engaging in personal matters that may feel offensive or like an invasion of privacy. Make it enjoyable, especially when the other person freely participates in the conversation.

Immediate surroundings

Another excellent small talk topic can be generated by observing what is around you and your partner. That is, you can quickly look around and comment on something that piques your interest. Some people may choose to compliment their partners on how they look, anything nice, or something they both have in common. This indicates that you will not be at a loss for words because your partner will undoubtedly understand what you are saying. Everyone enjoys a good compliment, especially when it is directed at their appearance. "I love your dress today; it pulls your outfit together," for example.

Interests

People with similar interests usually have something in common that brings them together, so it's important to develop small talk. In other words, it implies that you have a topic to discuss despite the absence of a specific topic. The interest could be anything from a mutual friend to a hobby that you both enjoy and participate in regularly. However, it is uncommon to ask someone about their hobbies because it sounds unnatural and awkward. Instead, ask based on observations that easily drive the point of what they enjoy doing. "I noticed you have a New York Giants logo," for example. "Do you enjoy American football?"

Approach and Mindset

Having a reason for small talk with people consists of developing self-confidence, which allows you to develop an exciting personality as well as interactive discussion Furthermore, it determines the progression of your interaction because inappropriate small talk indicates one answer response and the end of the discussion. Some people may now choose to remain silent until a meaningful topic is introduced. That is, the extent of the conversation is determined by your first impression.

Others, on the other hand, face the challenge of maintaining a positive attitude to initiate pleasant small talk with others.

Because the success of the topic is dependent on the first statement, your mindset may jeopardize the entire process, thus affecting the first impression. The mindset has been defined as a set of beliefs and thoughts held by one or more people, with a focus on life philosophy. As a result, your mindset can influence how you interact in a variety of ways. Among these are thoughts on how your topic might be perceived by your partner, group, or the person you meet. Your mindset can also boost your self-esteem by encouraging you to engage in small talk.

DEVELOPING A POSITIVE ATTITUDE

Overcoming Negative Thinking

Our daily activities usually shape our mindset, eliciting an emotional response that is necessary for both our quality of life and our mental health. Acquiring a stable state of mind can be difficult and can cause your mind to focus on the negatives instead. Negative thinking is one factor that lowers a person's self-esteem and self-love, resulting in significant life problems. The best way to cultivate a positive mindset is to confront the negatives within you. You should begin by identifying these negative thoughts using techniques such as cognitive behavioral therapy, mindfulness and yoga, and meditation.

You can also keep a thought journal to remind yourself of the negatives in your life that are destroying your mindset.

Being conscious of negative emotions and thoughts about the experience puts you in a position to focus on the positives.

Never ignore the negatives that will haunt you in the future; instead, replace them with positive thoughts. In this case, keep a gratitude journal alongside the negative journal you started earlier. Keep track of the best moments as well as instances that inspire your inner self. To that end, keep practicing positive imagery and maintaining your focus to keep the negative thoughts at bay while keeping you focused on the benefits of achieving greatness.

Improve Prospects

Another important technique for developing a positive mindset is to improve your outlook, which builds your positive thinking and improves your mindset. Life is full of challenges, and the best way to live happily is to focus on the good and avoid the bad. Regardless of how difficult the experience may be, look for the positives and capitalize on them. Though you will encounter these frustrations along the way, ensure that you change your reaction to them so that you do not feel as if you are experiencing the worst.

Take some time to relax, feel the airflow, and clear your mind, which will quickly change your inner thoughts.

The media has been identified as one of the primary causes of negative thinking, with individuals developing a negative mindset as a result of comparisons and negative comments on social media platforms. If you believe that this is another source of negative thinking, avoid media and instead do something you enjoy, such as drawing, sports, or painting.

Negative thinking has also been linked to a lack of efficacy and failures. Another way to improve your outlook is to try to become more humorous by having more fun and laughing with friends and family.

Engage in Interactive Activities

It is difficult to maintain a positive attitude when you are constantly alone and have no friends to talk to about something constructive. Furthermore, you are likely to be swept away by negative thoughts.

In various ways, it significantly damages your mindset. As a result, surrounding yourself with people who are always positive is the best way to boost your positive mindset. Positive people tend to transform negative behaviors into positive ones while promoting your way of thinking. Be positive toward others while showing interest and pride in them. This not only aids in the development of your mindset but also encourages others to associate with you.

It is also critical to take note when you lend a helping hand to others who are feeling helpless or low. According to studies, emphasizing your assistance to those in need makes you feel gratuitous, making you feel as if you contributed to society. You can also join social groups comprised of happy and positive-thinking people to be more interactive in developing your mindset. In most cases, religious and charitable organizations are among the best to associate with to cultivate a positive mindset.

Maintain a Healthy Lifestyle

Lifestyle has been linked to influencing various mental behaviors and emotions, and the mindset is no exception.

When you live a healthy and relaxing lifestyle, you are less likely to be susceptible to destroying your mindset. That is, getting enough sleep puts you in the forefront for your body to recover from frustration, which hurts your mindset. You gradually develop a more productive and positive mindset, which is required for comprehensive thinking. Eating well, drinking plenty of water, and exercising regularly can all help you develop a positive mindset. Embrace life while remembering that you are in control of your life and loving yourself unconditionally.

GENERAL GUIDELINES FOR MAKING GOOD SMALL TALK

Perform Some Homework

It's difficult to engage or start small talk if you don't know what the basics are, or what it entails. When you start by understanding the fundamentals of your desired topic, you are more likely to have a fruitful conversation with your partner. For example, if you want to discuss the Oscars, you must first do some research on the winners and those who were nominated but never won. If you choose to engage with the topic without doing any homework, you will most likely be embarrassed.

Appropriately Greet

Nothing shows your confidence more than greeting people firmly and with a smile on your face. Understand that small talks cover broad topics, and the response can be positive or negative with brief responses. However, if greetings are accompanied by a confident demeanor and a sense of humor, developing a conversation becomes a little easier. However, there are times when you must make small talk with familiar faces. As a result, you may even hug or kiss here, which contributes to the development of your conversation.

Keep Names in Mind

Though it may appear difficult, remembering names is extremely beneficial, especially when creating a successful stall talk. Introductions are usually brief and sometimes hurried because both parties discuss a variety of topics, making it difficult to remember names. When in a conversation, try to remember the names of these people, especially if they are new to you. Allow yourself some leeway in case someone mumbles; ask them to repeat the name so you get it right.

However, there are times when you may forget these names. As a result, you can either ask a third party or listen for it if it comes up in the conversation.

Rekindle Discussions

There are times when conversations end in silence, with all parties remaining silent. In this case, you may choose to restart the discussion and make it more interactive. Remember that silence does not always indicate that a topic has died, which is why it must be revived. In some cases, your partner may need some time to process the information before providing the necessary response. Furthermore, be cautious when reviving conversations, as some silences may serve as appropriate transitions for any discussion. Furthermore, be relaxed when establishing the topic to avoid sounding like an idiot babbling on about various topics.

Have Effective Introductions

When you decide to introduce yourself, especially to strangers, make sure you use an appropriate introduction that steers your conversation in the right direction. Accompany your name with information that, in most cases, will facilitate a discussion. Names in groups can be difficult, especially if you forget one or more names. However, you should not be concerned because you can quickly pick the names during the conversation or ask a third party. You can get the name quickly by pointing at the person and making it sound like you want to use her name as an example or just leave the topic to them.

End Conversations Properly

When it comes to ending a conversation after learning about each other, the best way to go is to end the meeting on a positive note with no issues. If there is a misunderstanding, do everything you can to diffuse it and create a peaceful environment between you.

Furthermore, end interactions with a smile and, if necessary, exchange contact information. Never let interactions end in an argument because it reduces the likelihood of another meeting.

A Small Talk's First Impression

As previously stated, a person's first impression may become a popular topic for starting a conversation. The situation in which one encounters another individual, object, or scene and forms a mental image of the same is defined as a first impression. That is, noticing specific characteristics that are familiar to you, or rather, imagining and creating with your visuals. Age, language, physical appearance, gender, posture, and voice are all factors that influence first impressions. First impressions have been linked to a variety of advantages, including determining the effectiveness of an object or scene as well as success when interacting with different people.

In small talk, first impressions are linked to having honest and successful conversations about complimenting your party's items. For example, you can make a conclusive statement about a group or your partner that makes them feel appreciated and loved. You are more likely to have a successful small talk with a limited chaotic outcome in this case. Similarly, an individual's mindset can be easily influenced, either positively or negatively, depending on how they interpret their first impression of a given entity.

Social Anxiety and Nerves

When an individual's nerves and anxiety behaviors are mentioned, it refers to the inner self of how an individual is capable of handling themselves in a situation. In other words, it refers to how you conduct yourself before making your first small talk with your audience. Nerves are interconnected fibers and axons that allow the body to respond appropriately to an external stimulus. In this case, social anxiety is an external stimulus caused by how you react when faced with social communication difficulties. Even though the behavior is a mental disorder, there are numerous techniques for dealing with such emotions.

For example, if you need to start small talk with your partner, group, or stranger, you may feel some internal resistance.

Your anxiety may cause you to fail to communicate, resulting in you remaining silent throughout. In some cases, you may feel the need to speak, but you find yourself shaking, sweating, breathing quickly, and even confused. These are internal symptoms of social anxiety. However, your symptoms are the result of your nervous system sensing your anxiety and attempting to protect you from speaking up and embarrassing yourself.

CHAPTER 2

The Importance of Small Talk

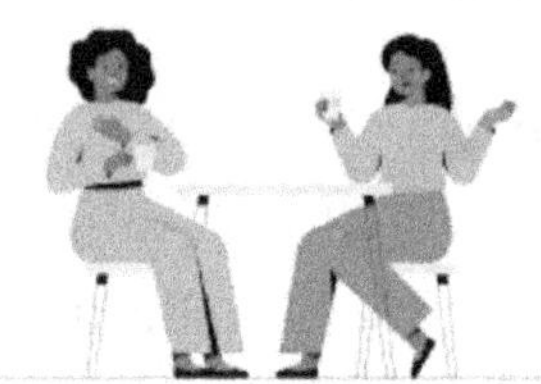

Every relationship or contact we wish to establish and maintain requires a method of exchanging information, i.e., effective communication. Communication allows us to express our emotions, perceptions, and preferences. As a result, to extract vital information that will assist you in making decisions and maintaining your friendship, you must initiate a conversation with the other party.

Small talk is a method of starting a conversation with people that allows you to maintain long-term relationships with friends, colleagues, and business associates. Small talk is intended to foster closeness and possibly intimacy by sharing your experiences, tastes, preferences, and overall feelings about something. You could talk about the weather, a popular movie or film, cultural events, inspirational books, breaking news, career choices, and a variety of other topics.

When a client like you, they are more likely to do business with you. People will not like your products or services if they do not like you. However, if you engage them in small talk and share your perceptions and how you make your preferences, you will most likely win the client over. Similarly, during the conversation, you can establish that you have a common background with the clients, which gives them a sense of belonging. However, you should keep the topic of discussion in mind. Some of the conversations may make the client feel uneasy. A suitable small talk will build trust in your clients and, eventually, loyalty.

You must express your preferences in personal relationships with your loved ones. Similarly, you can offer suggestions and opinions on a specific topic. Small talk can be used to express your feelings about your partner's behavior. Similarly, small talk can be used to enlighten the partners in a conversation about various niches in which you are well versed, for example, you could talk about an inspirational book you recently read.

WHY BOTHER WITH SMALL TALK?

It is reasonable to wonder why you should incorporate small talk into your relationship. Small talk is perceived as an additional activity that aids in gaining the partner's loyalty and trust. Small talk, on the other hand, is not an optional activity; rather, it is an essential tool for engaging your partner. Small talk can elicit friendship from strangers; similarly, it can aid in persuading the client that your products or services are the best fit.

The success of someone who uses small talk techniques cannot be compared to the success of someone who does things normally. Small talks, for example, involve more than one party, and thus different opinions and feedback can be gathered when compared to doing business the traditional way. Here are some responses to the question, "Why small talk?" The responses apply to both business and personal relationships.

Small Talk Improves Perception: Because small talk is mutual, you will have the opportunity to understand how others perceive things. Similarly, you will receive feedback on how you perceive things, which will aid in your personal development.

Small Talk Increases Bargaining Power: Sometimes simply expressing yourself is enough to persuade an unwilling customer. Small talk allows for mutual activities such as sharing ideas and discussing how to respond to specific issues.

The client will gain trust in you if you provide a solution.

Similarly, if you are the party in need of services or signage, small talk will help you understand the potential benefits and drawbacks of the activity in question. An excellent experience can assist you in obtaining a business contract that you may have thought was difficult to obtain.

Small Talks Improve Creativity: Small talks involve the discussion of various phenomena, issues, and facts.

As a result, your partner's argument will open your eyes to learn more than you could have done alone. For example, if the conversation is about literary works, your partner may provide an interpretation that you could not have figured out on your own. Similarly, discussing emerging issues will keep you up to date on current trends.

Small Talk Can Help You Show Your Admiration for Others: It is nearly impossible to persuade people who dislike you. If a person dislikes you, he or she will not listen to your ideas. Similarly, you cannot form a relationship with someone who dislikes you. However, a person may have disliked you because of rumors or malicious conversations. Small talk not only allows for information exchange but also shows how much you value and respect your partner. A person will like you because of your confidence and generosity, and because you cannot read like a book, you will have to initiate conversation.

Small Talks Aid in Identifying Your Potential: Psychologists have proven that each individual has a unique capability and gift. The possessed potential will not be recognized unless you begin working in the relevant field. For example, you may have firm argumentative skills that will help you make an effective advocate. You may be unaware, but the more you interact with people, the more they will notice your potential.

Small Talks are unavoidable, as is communication:

Communication is a means of exchanging information, which we cannot deny. Small talk is a way to express how you perceive things, your feelings about various niches, and your choices and preferences. As a result, when making decisions such as career choices and operations strategy, you must engage in small talk.

Human Interaction Foundations

There is an established interaction between the environment and the ecosystem in all living things, including humans. Social interaction refers to the actions that occur between people; in most cases, the actions are dictated by interactions with others.

People's interactions define the fundamentals of social structure; thus, the interaction can be used in social inquiry and analysis.

There are two types of social interaction: dyads and triads.

Triads are interactions between two groups, whereas triads are interactions between three or more social groups.

Social interaction shapes societal norms and cultural activities. Communities design ways to create a hospitable living environment through social interaction. Culture and societal norms represent the types of interactions that a given community expects. As a result, social interactions shape the lives of members of a given society.

COMMUNICATION FUNDAMENTALS

Communication is essential for human interaction with the environment, fellow humans, and the ecosystem. Sharing ideas, feelings, and perceptions is what communication entails. As a result, communication becomes unavoidable.

To live in harmony with other members of society, one must use effective communication skills to understand and share ideas with them.

Miscommunications result from a lack of effective communication skills. Most counseling experts admit that most couples seek their services because they lack communication skills. As a result, the only advice they can give is to educate the couple on how to communicate more effectively. This demonstrates the importance of having and using effective communication skills to live a more harmonious life. The following is a discussion of the communication bases, which are necessary for effective communication.

There are four major entities in communication.

1. The Originator

The person who encodes the message is referred to as the sender. To avoid misinterpretation, the sender should ensure that the message is precise. Similarly, because the sender initiates the communication cycle, much is expected of him or her.

2. The Key Message

The message denotes the specific information that the sender wishes to convey. However, the message can be delivered in a variety of ways. The most common formats are written, oral, and/or nonverbal.

3. The Canal

The medium used to connect the sender and receiver in the conveyance of the message is referred to as the channel.

Depending on the message and the audience, the sender should select an appropriate channel.

4. The Recipient

The audience to whom the message is addressed is referred to as the receiver. The receiver decodes the message to determine its meaning and can then respond by providing feedback to the sender via a channel.

Why Do Most Communication Attempts Fail?

If certain factors are not observed, information exchange via various channels may fail to achieve the intended goal.

Failure to convey the appropriate message can be caused by the following issues.

Inappropriate Message Encoding

Words are symbols of the actual meaning that was intended to be made in any communication. Because encoding is the first phase of communication, hiccups in this phase can affect all subsequent phases. As a result, when communicating, the choice of words, channel, and presentation characteristics should be highly valued. A lengthy message, for example, may elicit different reactions from different recipients. As a result, most recipients are unlikely to take the time to go through the entire presentation. As a result, the message should be encoded in as concise and comprehensive a manner as possible.

Similarly, the message should be tailored to the audience, as ambiguity will result from vagueness. When the receiver is unable to understand the message, the interpretation is likely to deviate from the intended. Similarly, the message should be leveled according to the receivers' expectations. For example, the language used in a message aimed at doctors cannot be the same as that used in a message aimed at students or farmers. At some point, the sender may have complex ideas that can only be decoded correctly by people on his or her level. As a result, the message should be simple while still incorporating the keywords to avoid meaning loss.

Inappropriate Message Decoding

To some extent, the sender can overcome the challenge of misinterpretation by communicating comprehensively and concisely. However, depending on the stored knowledge, the receiver may misinterpret the message. The most common causes of interpretation are a lack of keenness, ineffective decoding skills, and when the receiver interprets in a biased manner by assuming meanings other than those intended.

As a result, the receiver must pay close attention to every aspect of the communication. For example, if the communication is verbal, the receiver should pay attention to nonverbal cues and tonal variation.

EFFECTIVE COMMUNICATION TECHNIQUES

After discussing the barriers to effective communication, you should now learn how to communicate effectively. If you are the sender, effective communication means that you will deliver the message in a way that your audience will understand. Effective communication, on the other hand, means being able to interpret and attach the appropriate meaning to the message if you are a receiver.

Recognize Your Weaknesses

You may not be able to follow every principle to achieve effective communication. As a result, you should be well aware of your flaws and the consequences.

For example, you may not be fluent in the language of presentation. In such cases, you may want to include nonverbal and visual communication as well.

Select the Best Vocabulary and Presentation Format

The message's technicality can influence the receiver's interpretation. Understand your audience before presenting your message. When communicating with doctors, for example, you should use a higher level while using specific words. When communicating with people who have lower intelligence, however, modify the communication to make the message more comprehensive.

Request for Audience Feedback

You may believe that your message is being received, but this may not be the case. As a result, solicit feedback from your audience on how they interpret the message.

Similarly, when communicating in front of an audience, you should pay attention to their reactions and behaviors. For example, agitation indicates that the

The audience is either unfamiliar with the topic under discussion or the message itself is incomprehensible.

Clarification Request from the Sender

If you are on the receiving end, the main challenge is correctly decoding the message. As a result, if any details are unclear, request clarification from the sender.

Introvert versus Extrovert

People have different personalities; for example, some are humbled while others are proud. However, distinct personalities can be divided into two categories: introverts and extroverts. Introverted people are reserved and focused on their thoughts; they rarely open up. Extroverts, on the other hand, are people who are very social, talkative, more open, and easily befriended. The following are the primary distinctions between introverts and extroverts.

Introverts prefer to be alone or with a small group of close friends; they are also, in most cases, overthinkers. Extroverts, on the other hand, are talkative and outspoken individuals who enjoy conversing with those around them.

Introverts are known to be reserved and self-sufficient. Extroverts, on the other hand, are welcoming and friendly.

Introverts are more considerate when communicating. They pause before speaking. Extroverts, on the other hand, express their true feelings; they talk a lot, especially when they want to learn more about something.

Introverts are self-motivated and do not rely on external factors for motivation. Extroverts, on the other hand, feel motivated when they are with their social partners.

Introverts are more time conscious and enjoy spending time alone; as a result, they avoid social situations.

Extroverts, on the other hand, are socialites who enjoy spending time with their friends, family, and colleagues.

Introverts believe in meditating and internally synthesizing solutions to problems. Extroverts, on the other hand, solve their problems by soliciting feedback from others.

Introverts are excellent secret keepers; they rarely open up only to those they trust. As a result, they prefer to keep their social circle small. Extroverts, on the other hand, believe in popularity and, as a result, see engaging with a large number of people as a success.

Introverts are resistant to change because they are slow to adapt. Extroverts, on the other hand, readily accept change and enjoy having an 'updated' status.

Introverts have a high level of concentration and do not easily lose focus. Extroverts, on the other hand, are easily distracted and cannot concentrate for long periods.

BODY LANGUAGE AND NONVERBAL COMMUNICATION

As previously stated, a message can be delivered in one of three ways: written, oral, or nonverbal. However, the formats can be mutually dependent at times. Nonverbal communication is the element of communication that is not spoken. Body language, on the other hand, is a type of nonverbal communication that entails distinct movement and physical behavior that is intended to express a specific message.

Gestures, body posture, and tonal variation are all examples of body language elements.

Understanding the entire communication requires the ability to deduce the meaning of nonverbal communication. To begin, nonverbal communication can be used to indicate when a communicator is emphasizing a specific point. Similarly, nonverbal communication can be used to establish the message's authenticity; that is, you can tell when someone is lying. Nonverbal communication, on the other hand, can serve as audience feedback.

For example, restlessness indicates a lack of concentration, whereas leaning forward indicates eagerness.

How to Spot Negatives

Emotions and feelings are necessary for effective communication. As a result, understanding characteristics that can help you detect unspoken issues or negative feelings is critical. The following are some aspects that can be used to detect negations.

The conversation is difficult, and there is a lot of defensiveness.

When a person stammers or uses ambiguous communication, they may be concealing information or are uncomfortable making a specific communication. Similarly, when a communication is made, the subject may defend himself or herself even before being prompted to do so.

Some activities, on the other hand, can help you determine whether or not the person(s) is/are interested. To begin, if the person turns away from you, it indicates discomfort and uneasiness. Second, if the person makes little eye contact, it may indicate uneasiness.

Inability to concentrate

It is easy to detect disinterest in your audience when giving a presentation. Common nonverbal cues that a person is uninterested include the person facing down and peering through windows.

A person can be seen looking away from the presentation.

I was fidgeting and dragging my chair.

Minor activities include fiddling with pens and phones and doodling.

HOW TO USE NONVERBAL POSITIVE COMMUNICATION

Despite having different message presentation formats, they can be used independently. For example, for verbal communication to be effective, it should be accompanied by nonverbal communication. However, you must ensure that you connect the most appropriate nonverbal.

Be at ease.

Relaxation implies that you are confident in what you are saying. As a result, be at ease when communicating; sit or stand upright with your hands by your sides (do not put them in your pocket). Similarly, do not place your hands on your hips as this indicates aggression or dominance.

Make a firm handshake.

Psychologists have discovered that a handshake can reveal a lot. To begin with, a sloppy handshake indicates awkwardness or a lack of confidence. As a result, when prompted, use a firm handshake.

Maintain Visual Contact

Eye contact demonstrates your confidence and certainty in the message you are conveying. Throughout the presentation, maintain eye contact with the other person or the audience. However, do not stare at them as this will make them feel uneasy. Staring at someone causes him or her to believe that he or she has made a mistake, which causes discomfort as he or she attempts to locate the error.

You must not scratch your head or touch your face.

Scratching your head indicates that you are cooking whatever you want to say. The primary causes are that you are unfamiliar with the issue at hand, as is the case with touching your face. If you are asked to respond to an issue about which you are unsure, simply state that you do not know. Otherwise, scratching your head and touching your face indicates that whatever you're trying to say is invalid or diluted.

CHAPTER 3

How to Improve Your Social Skills

What distinguishes humans from other lower animals is their ability to communicate and form friendships through language.

People interact to meet various needs through communication. Social skills are what allow a person to communicate and interact with others. This article will provide you with useful tips on how to improve your social skills, set goals, the importance of empathy, and meet people and make friends.

The article will also provide useful information on understanding yourself and others.

THE MEANING AND IMPORTANCE OF SOCIAL SKILLS

Social skills are the abilities that enable people to communicate, interact, and form harmonious interpersonal relationships. The ability to communicate, influence, and build harmonious relationships are all components of social interaction. There are various levels of communication. Interpersonal communication, group communication, social media communication, and communication through mainstream media are examples of these.

Communication can also be divided into three types: written, verbal, and nonverbal. While written communication is the process of communicating through written symbols, verbal communication is the process of communicating through spoken words. When communicating orally, you are expected to use a variety of nonverbal cues. These are the cues, gestures, and facial expressions you use when speaking.

When it comes to communication, social skills are essential. Having these abilities allows you to interact with people effectively.

Furthermore, people will pay attention to your message if you have good social skills. Social skills provide numerous advantages. These are some examples:

1. Creating a friendly work environment - People with social skills can interact well with others and reduce conflict incidents. Leaders with social skills can understand others and use persuasive techniques to persuade them.

2. Knowledge acquisition - When you have excellent social skills, you can interact with people from all walks of life and learn a lot. The knowledge you gain will help you to reduce conflict.

3. Network Expansion - If you have good social skills, you will be able to communicate with people from all walks of life. Some of these people may have opportunities that will help you improve your financial situation.

4. Providing your perspectives - When you have excellent social skills, you can provide your perspectives on various issues. These points of view may be useful to others.

5. Focused - With social skills, you can become focused on achieving shared goals.

6. Business expansion - When you have admirable social skills, people will say nice things about you, which may entice others to use your services. You're more likely to expand your business through referrals than through advertising.

SOCIAL SKILLS ENHANCING QUALITIES

Social skills are necessary for anyone who wishes to be successful in life. This is because these abilities assist us in developing and maintaining relationships. If you want to improve your social skills, you should adopt a variety of characteristics. These are the following:

1. Effective Communication - Communication is an important aspect of social skills. Communication will help you to effectively articulate your thoughts and bring them to the forefront. When you're good at communication, you can put together a team to accomplish something.

2. Conflict resolution - Conflicts can arise in any social environment. You can resolve these conflicts peacefully if you are a leader with excellent social skills.

3. Active listening entails paying close attention to what is being said. When you pay attention to the other party, they will respect you greatly. There are several strategies you can use to become an active listener. These include avoiding distractions, focusing on what is said, and preparing to comment or ask questions.

4. Empathy - Empathy allows you to put yourself in the shoes of others and identify with their feelings. An empathic person carefully considers the feelings of others. You can build strong relationships with others by honing your empathetic skills.

5. Relationship Management - Social skills are necessary for successful relationship management. When you manage a relationship, you can connect with specific clients and form strong bonds with them.

6. Respect - Respect is an important aspect of communication. When you respect others, you can let them speak without interruption. You also show your appreciation for others when you communicate by asking thoughtful and relevant questions, staying on topic, and not wasting time.

Improving Your Social Skills Strategies

1. Seeking Feedback - You can improve your social skills by asking your closest friends and colleagues to advise you on areas where you should improve. You should choose genuine feedback and apply it to improve your social skills.

2. Set Goals - Once you've identified your areas for improvement, you must devise a plan for how to improve yourself. Make sure to include specific and measurable goals in your proposal.

3. Locate Resources - There are numerous resources available to help you improve your social skills. These activities include using the internet, reading relevant books, and attending specific classes.

4. Practice - Once you've learned the various strategies for improving your social skills, it's critical that you put what you've learned into action. You can begin working out at home or work.

5. Continue Learning - The key to maintaining your social skills is to continue learning.

How to Set Objectives

Every aspect of what we do necessitates a strategy. When there are clear goals, these plans can be carried out. Goals are specific objectives that you hope to achieve when doing something. There are several steps that you must take if you want to be successful with goal setting.

This section provides helpful hints on how to set goals in whatever plans you have.

1. Write them down - You can't have anything that you can call a goal if you don't write it down. What is in your head cannot be called a target until it is written down. The purpose of writing down goals is to make them concrete making them more memorable You can easily lose sight of goals that are in your head.

2. Be Specific About Goals - In addition to writing them down, goals must be specific. When goals are precise, they are measurable, and their progression can be monitored. Specific goals are concrete and written in simple terms.

3. Specific Timeframe - It is critical to be specific about when you expect to achieve your goals. When you specify the date, month, and year of your goal's completion, you become more focused on working towards it. It is critical to use a calendar and set a realistic timeframe for achieving the goal.

4. Why you want to achieve the goal - It's critical to understand why you have the goal and why you want to achieve it. You must have a compelling reason why you have the goal. For example, going to the gym could help you lose weight and improve your health. When you have a reason for creating a goal, you become more committed to achieving it.

5. Goals should be measurable - When developing goals, make sure they are measurable so you can track your progress toward achieving them. There should be a specific metric that will help you track the progress of your goals. For example, if you want to lose 50kgs in five months, you should aim to reduce your load by 10kgs per month. When you set measurable goals for yourself, it is much easier to track your progress and work toward achieving them.

6. MAP (Massive Action Plan) - A massive action plan is a detailed plan for achieving your goals. The plan includes tactics, methods, and techniques for achieving your goal. In other words, your MAP should provide an answer to the question of how. For example, if you want to lose 50kgs in five months, you should outline the methods and strategies you'll use. Going to the gym and dieting are two examples.

7. Recognize Limiting Beliefs - You may have limiting beliefs that are impeding your goal achievement strategy. You must recognize and work to overcome these limiting beliefs. For example, suppose you're a single woman looking for a reliable male partner for marriage. Your assumption, on the other hand, is that all men are liars. This limiting belief should be removed from your goal-attainment strategy. It is critical to write down all of the limiting beliefs and devise a strategy for eliminating them.

8. Mental objections - In addition to limiting beliefs, you must be prepared to wrestle with spiritual objections. Psychological complaints are ideas that we have formed in our heads after hearing what our friends say. For example, a friend may tell you that losing weight is difficult and will take up a lot of your time. If you want to lose weight, you need to get rid of this mindset so it doesn't hold you back.

9. Time management - You cannot achieve your goals if you do not effectively manage your time. Setting aside time to work on your goals is critical. During this time, avoid time wasters and any other unnecessary distractions. You can use time management tools that are available on the internet.

10. Tracking your performance - You need to have a system of evaluating your progress toward goal achievement. For instance, you can break your bigger goals into smaller bits so that you easily track how you're progressing on a daily, weekly, or monthly basis. For instance, if your goal is to lose 50kgs at the end of 5 months,

you need to have a system of tracking whether you are losing 10kgs every month.

HOW TO IMPROVE YOUR EMPATHY

Empathy is the ability to identify with other people's feelings. An empathetic person can understand another person's feelings and offer a solution. There are various components of empathy that \ you need to develop. These are some examples:

1. Listening skills - An empathetic person has good listening skills. When you have excellent listening skills, it means that you don't interrupt others when they're talking, you ask relevant questions and make well-thought comments. It's essential to learn to be empathetic as people will confide in you.

2. Attentiveness - Being attentive means that you get more focused on listening to what the other person is saying. It would be best to avoid any distractions that will make you not be able to listen attentively. You should also avoid interrupting the other party when they're talking.

3. Appreciate other people's cultures - You develop empathetic skills when you learn to respect other people's sculptures. This requires that you travel a lot to meet new people from diverse cultural backgrounds. When you understand the reasons why people

behave the way they do, you'll be empathetic and learn to appreciate them without any biases.

4. Request for feedback - It's advisable to request your close friends offer you suggestions on how you should enhance your listening skills. After getting the feedback, come up with a strategy for implementing the recommendations. It would be best if you also learned to practice various aspects that you're enhancing.

5. Reading – Different books explore the topic of empathy. It's essential to look for these books and read them to improve your empathy skills. You can also look for valuable materials on the internet that shed light on the subject of empathy.

6. Evaluate your biases - To be able to be empathetic, it's essential to examine the biases that we have about others, which prevent us from listening to them empathetically.

    Maybe you're biased against somebody because of their race, color, or gender. When you remove these biases, you'll improve your empathetic skills.

7. Be curious - when you're curious, you need to listen to other people's stories regardless of their background. This curiosity will enable you to improve your empathy because you'll take the time to listen to people you would never have heard in the first place.

8. Frame the right questions - The kind of questions that you ask will determine the amount of empathy that you'll display. It's essential to learn to ask the right questions that are relevant to the subject under discussion.

STEPS OF GETTING NEW FRIENDS

You're likely to meet new faces most of the time. It's essential to develop skills on how we should start, nurture, and develop new relationships. This section offers you tips on how to make new friends.

1. Your fear is baseless - Some people feel scared about the likelihood of meeting new people. They will take much time to think about what they'll tell these new people and what thoughts the new individuals will form about them. In other words, the prospect of meeting new people is scary. However, it's essential to discover that your fear is unsubstantiated and is only serving to prevent new friends from coming into your life.

2. Learn to start small - In case you're scared of meeting new people that you'll socialize with and become good friends with, it's advisable that you start low with the people that you know. In this regard, it's essential to start with your friend's friends, your acquaintances, and accept invitations for going out. When you start with the people you know, you'll begin developing self-confidence in meeting people that you've never met the whole of your life.

3. Move out now - After you've reinforced the friendship ties with your inner friends, it's now time to move out and meet new faces.

You can accomplish this goal through meetups, attending workshops, volunteering, and going to parties, clubs, and others. Meetup groups enable you to meet people that have the same interest as yours. For example, you can have a meetup of people who're interested in cycling or online marketing. Workshops offer training opportunities for people interested in specific areas like research. It's essential to find out when a workshop that you're interested in may start so that you can attend and create new friends.

4. Take the first step - The first step is to greet somebody and introduce yourself to them. Tell the other party what you do in life and then offer them an opportunity to say something too. At first, avoid moving into complex subjects but ask them simple things like how they found specific topics in the workshop.

5. Be open Minded - It's essential to open your mind when you see new faces out there and avoid the tendency to prejudge them. You should always let some time pass before you start judging people. For instance, in case you would like a friend who loves traveling to new places but thinks that the one you've just met doesn't, it's essential to give them time before you start judging them. Maybe, you may arouse their interest, and they may start moving out. In the same breath, it's also essential to open your heart to the other party. This means that you start trusting them and believing that they're good friends of yours.

6. Understand the person - As you develop your friendship, it's important to start knowing the other person well for a great connection. You need to know what they do, their hobbies, and other things.

CHAPTER 4

How to Begin a Conversation

A conversation is defined as interactive communication between two or more people. A conversation is defined as two or more people talking together. It is a type of speech that occurs symmetrically and informally, to establish and maintain social ties. Conversations necessitate listening and providing feedback.

Conversations are considered social interactions; thus, they adhere to certain etiquette rules and vary depending on the social situation. Communication rules are based on the cooperative principle.

Failure to adhere to the standards causes a conversation to deteriorate and, in some cases, to end. The cooperative principle in conversations is classified into four maxims. To improve effective communication, the four categories are used to describe rational principles followed by individuals who adhere to the cooperative policy.

Quality Maxim - It is made up of supermaxims and submaxims. Supermaxim encourages people to be genuine in their contributions to a conversation. Submaxims also encourage people to avoid communicating what they believe to be false and to avoid saying things for which they lack sufficient evidence. The quality maxim ensures that people make contributions that are far more informative about the current reason for communication. Furthermore, people should avoid making contributions that are more informative than necessary.

Maxim of Relationship/Relevance - During a conversation, one should maintain relevance. Contributions should be made that are relevant to communication, and changes should be made only when necessary.

Manner Maxim - The supermaxim requires one to be perceptive, whereas the submaxim requires one to avoid ambiguity, and vagueness of expression, and to be as brief and orderly as possible.

The maxims listed above provide important guidelines for effective communication. Contributions made in a conversation should be entirely dependent on what has already been saying.

CONVERSATION TYPES

When conversing with another person, it is critical to understand the type of conversation you two are having. You can easily understand this by looking at the direction and tone of the communication you are having. Conversations can be classified into four major types based on their direction and tone. There are four of them: debate, dialogue, discourse, and diatribe.

A debate is defined as a competitive, two-way conversation. The main goal of such a conversation is to win an argument or persuade others. Consider two university students from opposing political parties arguing about politics.

Dialogue - Dialogue is a cooperative two-way conversation. The primary goal of dialogue is to exchange information and foster healthy relationships between two or more people. A dialogue example would be two undecided university students communicating with each other to identify the best student leaders to vote for.

Discourse is one-sided and cooperative communication.

The primary goal of such a discussion is to convey information from a writer or speaker to readers or listeners. A professor giving a lecture on public administration to students is an example of a discourse conversation.

Diatribe - This is a competitive one-way communication. The conversation's goal is to express emotions, browbeating people who disagree with you, or inspiring people who share your viewpoints. As an example, consider a student discussing the results of the elections for student leaders.

Understanding the four types of conversations allows you to determine the type of communication you are having and thus the function of the conversation. Identifying the purpose of a conversation allows you to speak about the topics that are important to you. Misidentification leads to conversational stumbling blocks, where the conversation loses focus and eventually ends.

STARTING A DISCUSSION

Conversations are viewed as social constructs that aid in the formation and maintenance of relationships. It could include a basic dialogue in which people communicate their thoughts and ideas to others.

Conversations provide opportunities to learn new ideas while also presenting your information.

When you need to speak with a professional or a stranger, you may not have enough time to consider the terms and patterns of a conversation. Unlike when you are excitedly talking to a friend or relative about a song you are about to release, a stranger may believe you are trying to convince them to buy the song. You should be able to steer a conversation in the direction you want it to go a skilled conversationalist. The following are seven methods for starting and directing a conversation.

Begin with weather or sports-related topic - small talk may elicit feelings of hatred; however, it is the best way to start a conversation that does not commit to a specific topic.

Beginning a conversation with the weather or sports gives you several options for steering the conversation in some direction. You could mention a game you used to play in high school or how you are looking forward to a change in the weather.

You could begin by mentioning how hot the weather is as well as how the upcoming season will allow you to take a vacation and explore the coasts.

Making a Compliment - Compliments are a great way to start a conversation. This is because the recipient is flattered, which causes them to warm up to you and feel comfortable engaging in conversation with you. Before you give a compliment, make sure it is genuine and specific.

This will help you avoid alienating the person receiving the compliment. Allow the recipient of the compliment to provide feedback on the source of the compliment. This way, you will discover that you have exhausted the topic, allowing you to come up with another relevant topic. Your partner will be more willing to listen to you, and you will have an amazing conversation.

Talking about the Environment - The environment you're in can be a great conversation starter. For example, at a networking event, you can discuss the seating or the coffee; in an office, you can discuss the changes in room construction. In this case, the most important thing is to find something in your surroundings that your partner can also find. If both of you are sympathetic to the situation, you are likely to engage in a conversation about the nature of the environment. When you've exhausted the environment topic, you can switch gears by thinking of another activity in which your partner might be interested.

Asking for a Favour - As a psychological trick for starting conversations, Ben Franklin invented asking for a favor. When someone does you a favor, an inherent connection is formed. This is because they want to hear what you have to say and how you want to be assisted. The assistance does not have to be extensive; it can be as simple as asking where the restrooms are located. When someone assists you, you can quickly strike up a new conversation.

Opening with a Joke - Everyone enjoys jokes.

When you want to start a conversation with someone else, tell a calm and intelligent joke that will make the other person smile, resulting in a sympathetic bond. The connection formed between you two can be maintained throughout the conversation. Before telling your joke, consider the type of conversation you want to have so that you can tell a joke about it. This way, you'll be able to steer the conversation in the direction you want it to go. A joke will also make the other person feel more comfortable talking to you.

Begin with an Inoffensive Observation - Any observation you make will help you start a conversation. It is, however, critical to consider discovering something that leads to your desired topic of conversation. You can do this simply by pointing something out and asking your partner what they like about it. A string of conversations will be introduced in this manner, and you will be able to direct it to your desired conversational goal.

Asking a Superficially Related Question to your Intended Topic - When people are asked specific questions, they are more likely to participate in the intended conversation. Asking questions that are not directly related to your intended topic of conversation will cause it to veer of course. Asking a question about the topic you're about to discuss allows your conversation partner to participate in the conversation openly. For example, if you're telling a friend about some new music you're about to release, you can ask if they've recently listened to any good music. This question will open the door for you to direct the conversation to your music. In this case, you must stay in the conversation and ask directory questions.

Listen to the responses until you are ready to introduce your intended topic. Avoid forcing a topic on someone because it will turn them off. It is also critical that you ask open-ended questions so that your partner can come up with multiple responses. The responses provided can also be used to initiate a new conversation topic.

Small Talk Tips and Tricks

You will most likely meet many new people if you are invited to events such as a community outing, a colleague's wedding, or a company party. When you realize that such situations necessitate small talk, you may become anxious rather than excited. Small talk does not have to be meaningless or involve insignificant communication. There are several ways to make small talk livelier and more engaging.

Getting Your Mind in Order - You may spend the majority of your time worrying about how you will feel in social situations. This way, you will have the mindset that you will fail at small talk. As a result, you should go in with the mindset that you are going to a celebration and that you will meet people with similar interests or interact with your colleagues. This way, you'll feel more at ease going to the event and engaging in any small talk that may arise.

Before you go to the event, decide whom you want to meet. This entails thinking about the people you'll be interacting with and those who may be sharing something with you. You might recall a fellow football fan or someone you saw a movie with. This will help you come up with some small talk topics to discuss.

Making it into a Game - Tricking your mind can help you see the conversation as more relaxed and enjoyable. You should always try to push yourself by learning new things. You can set a goal of meeting at least three people per day. You will be able to reduce anxiety and make small talk conversations more engaging by making such mental shifts.

Always strive to accept responsibility for Meeting Other People - If you want to gain the confidence to engage in small talk, don't sit around waiting for others to approach you. Always make an effort to be the first to greet the other person.

Other people's expectations of making the first move can be quite disappointing. As a result, consider accepting responsibility.

Avoid Always being the sidekick - Being able to engage in small talk necessitates attempting to meet new people on your own. You should not always expect to meet new people through someone you already know.

Always Show Interest by Listening to More Than You Talk - Asking questions is the secret tool for making small talk. Always ask open-ended questions and actively listen to your partner's response to find a topic for your conversation. You will notice that the questions you ask add substance to the conversation, turning it into a true conversation.

Be Yourself - Fake networking can put people off. It is critical that you remain true to yourself and do not try to be someone you are not. Always strive to present your true self.

Be an Introducer - During a conversation, you may notice another guest who appears to be uncomfortable. What you should do is invite them to your discussion. This will make it more interesting and livelier.

Read Up on Current Events - Keeping up with current events and news will always provide you with ideas for starting small talk. People will always want to hear what you have to say.

HOW TO MAINTAIN A CONVERSATION

Obstinate silence is one of the challenges you face when meeting new people at social gatherings. Such situations can make you feel uneasy, so you try to avoid social situations as much as possible. Failure to understand how to keep a conversation going can hurt your social life. On the other hand, if you know how to keep words flowing in a conversation, you can learn a lot about the people you like, which creates significant capabilities for healthy relationships and shared activities.

Reasons Why You Can't Think of Anything to Say in a Conversation

Several patterns of behavior can prevent you from having meaningful conversations with new people. One of the habits is filtering.

This is where you notice that you consistently avoid talking about something unless you check with yourself to make sure it is cool, interesting, impressive, or cool. The second issue is that it is difficult to get into a conversational mood. In this case, you have difficulty warming up and interacting with those around you. This behavior can cause you to sit around people for an entire day without being able to initiate or join in on their conversation.

Learning new skills and tips, on the other hand, can help you overcome the characteristics that make it difficult to keep words flowing in a conversation, transforming you into an incredible conversationalist.

There will be no filtering. You should try to express anything that is on your mind. Checking yourself to see if something is impressive or clever is not necessary. You can easily practice this technique by attempting it in front of people you know quite acquainted with Only avoid saying anything that could land you in jail. You will realize that speaking your mind will not result in people passing judgment on you. In most cases, people will be concerned with how they will convey what you are saying rather than how interesting it is.

Responding with Phrases that Encourage Your Partner to Continue Speaking - This technique is completely effective for keeping a conversation going. You can use phrases like "interesting, tell me more," or "wow, how did you go about it." When you show people that you are interested in what they are saying, they will stay and enjoy talking to you. The phrases you use during the conversation show your partner that you are interested in listening to them, which encourages them to keep talking to you.

Creating Stories from Anywhere - This is a very important technique for keeping a conversation going.

A discussion becomes more interesting when stories are added to it. You should try to tell stories from all walks of life rather than just your own. For example, you could discuss the experiences of other people you know or characters you've seen in magazines, on TV, or the radio.

When you first learn how to use stories, incorporating them into your conversation is simple. You have already experienced or heard the stories, so you are certain of them.

When your partner mentions something related to the account, you can tell them about it, which brings the conversation to life. People will be more open with you if you can share such stories with them.

The key to maintaining a conversation is to apply the guidelines to the person you meet. You should avoid overburdening yourself by using all of the tricks at once; instead, try each one at a different time.

Learning one tip increases your confidence as you attempt to apply other techniques in potential conversations.

EXITING A CONVERSATION

Despite how interesting a conversation is, you may need to end it before your partner is ready. As a result, you must end the conversation strategically without appearing rude. There are numerous ways to end a conversation diplomatically, including using words and indirectly using body language.

Here are some pointers to help you gracefully end a conversation.

Finally, a positive comment - Wrapping up a conversation with positive comments can help you end it on a high note. You can do this by thanking your fellow conversationalist for their time, indicating that you are ready to end the conversation. Things may seem to drag on for a long time at times, and you must wait for the other person to finish what they are saying. You can then smile at them and say things like, "I'm so grateful that you took the time to talk with us," or "thank you so much for your time." If your partner does not get the hint, you can say something like, "well, thank you again, but I need to get going."

Waiting for a Natural Pause in Conversation to Leave - Every conversation, no matter how interesting, has a natural pause. When you want to end a conversation, wait a few minutes and tell your partner things like, "wow, it's been incredible talking to you, but I should get going."

Making Long-Term Plans - Offering concrete plans is a good and courteous way to end a conversation. It will demonstrate to your partner that you enjoyed talking with them and would like to talk with them again. You must wait for the speaker to finish their sentence before saying things like, "What are you up to next weekend/Do you want to grab some wine?" You can also exchange contact information with the person and discuss exchanging e-mails or messages to make plans.

A conversation may appear to be simple to begin, continue, and end successfully; however, people must learn some techniques for having a great conversation. People should always strive to make the conversation as lively as possible, to foster friendships and new experiences.

CHAPTER 5

Persuasion Techniques

We all need to influence others from time to time, but we don't always know how. We have a sense of gaining trust and developing a relationship with others based on our influence rather than manipulating them, whether at work or anywhere else we are around people. Anyone can become a leader, but it is often difficult, especially when it comes to gaining people's respect and regard as a leader. Becoming a leader is a method of influencing others and gaining their trust. You've probably seen situations where someone has good qualities and is capable of delivering the best, but fails to advance because their rivals are elected by a large margin. This is always due to influence, as some people are better at influencing different people than others.

Influence is the ability to change someone's actions, thoughts, opinions, and decisions. This appears to be an impossible task based solely on the definition. That is, you may wonder how someone can get into your head and change the way you think.

However, the practice is possible, and great leaders use influence to gain others' respect, trust, and the position they hold. Influence essentially means compliance.

In other words, forcing someone to do what you want them to do.

Influence is all around us, and you can use it to make new friends or work effectively with new people without any authority. Influence is essential for various people to achieve their goals, motivations, and inspirations while ensuring that others are always on their side. Control without manipulation is a difficult process that is typically measurable, predictable, and repeatable. Even though both use the mind to change an individual's mental behaviors, influence and manipulation accompany significant differences.

INFLUENCE TYPES

Negative Impact

This is the polar opposite of positive influence and is usually the most damaging type of influence because those who engage in it are primarily concerned with power or authority over others. That is, these people are egocentric and proud, and they usually use force or tricks to get to the top. As a result, they are leaders, but they lack respect, and people find it difficult to follow and listen to them. As the title suggests, their outcomes are usually negative, hurting either the organization or the team. These leaders, moreover, fail to achieve any beneficial goal because the results produced are frequently insufficient. It is critical to remove or avoid such leaders because their motivation for leadership is usually harmful.

Neutral influence

Neutral influences are a leader's general practices and attitudes that have no positive or negative impact on others.

These leaders are typically neutral in nature and have little impact, making them stand out from the crowd. That is, they neither add nor subtract value from a company or team. They offer no assistance, take no action, or become proactive in any way. Despite having no advantages or disadvantages, these leaders typically sit back and wait for the staff or people under their leadership to take action and achieve specific goals because they are never influenced. This is another type to avoid because these leaders do nothing to advance their positions.

Positive Impact

Leaders are excellent examples of positive influence because they add value and work with happy people. This is a very useful type of influence, especially for leaders who are actively involved with people and take positive actions.

perspectives on others the positive aspect of this type is that the leader becomes the one who inspires, leads, and trains others to create and grow relationships with others. Being a positive influencer implies that you can quickly establish yourself as a mentor and assist others in becoming successful. Furthermore, this type of influence necessitates higher levels of intentionality, effort, and passion to ensure that everyone succeeds in life.

The influence that Changes Lives

This is the most valuable and zenith type of influence, and only a few people strive to achieve it.

Despite having a positive influence, becoming a leader takes years, if not decades, to master the skills required to lead well and change lives.

Life-changing influence, as opposed to positive influence, entails making decisions that permanently alter an individual's life through actions or words. Those you influence remain in a similar state even after the leader of an organization or team has passed away. Life-changing leaders typically devote their entire lives, time, and attention to assisting others in becoming successful, without regard for greed, pride, or the desire to meet their own needs. Oprah Winfrey, Mother Teresa, and Abraham Lincoln are among the life-changing influencers.

HOW TO PERSUADE OTHERS

Develop Relationships

Developing good relationships with others is the first step toward becoming a leader, especially if you want to make new friends. One way to start a good relationship is to have a friendlier and more outgoing personality, which influences others when they find you exciting and comfortable.

Take a genuine interest in others to make a good impression, and address them by name to make the message more personalized. Participating in an open Regular discussion builds trust by not forcing ideas but rather matching them on topics at hand.

Share what you have while discussing other people's interests, and remember to respect opposing viewpoints.

CREATE A POSITIVE REPUTATION

Another important aspect of persuading people is to establish a reputation that stands out from the crowd. This can be accomplished by always admitting mistakes when you are wrong and highlighting the wrongdoings of others in a logical, positive, indirect, and constructive manner. Furthermore, demonstrate your expertise in areas where you have extensive knowledge while engaging in activities that make people respect and admire your way of life. You can also build your reputation by demonstrating an eagerness to learn more with an open mind, whether from your seniors or through mistakes made along the way.

Helping Others

When it comes to influencing people, one of the most important things you can do is lend a helping hand in a variety of ways. One of them is to approach people in a more friendly manner. Never be bossy or demanding, as this demonstrates arrogance and a desire for power over others. Sympathize by demonstrating reciprocity in their beliefs and actions, which should be entirely positive. Encourage positive changes in society while avoiding giving commands and orders, which are usually considered disrespectful. Save those who are embarrassed by embracing those who propose ideas, making corrections, and allowing these ideas to be theirs.

Finally, instead of becoming envious of others, praise them. Allow them to be motivated by your generosity, but never praise them for the sake of making them feel good.

Communication Style Analysis

Learning communication styles is critical, especially for leaders to understand how they communicate and converse with others, More importantly, it enables people to understand how they interact with friends, family, and colleagues and make the necessary changes to have an active and assertive interaction. The same is true for those who can influence others; they always have the opportunity to communicate and share their ideas. There are various communication styles in which one can use one or more techniques when speaking in various situations.

Style of Assertion

This is the most effective communication style, and it is typically used by leaders with much higher self-esteem. It is one of the healthiest and employs all of the positive aspects of communication skills, including behavioral, language, verbal, and nonverbal techniques. Accepting compliments, taking responsibility for your actions, standing up for your rights while respecting those of others, and expressing yourself socially and emotionally are all examples of behavioral characteristics.

This language is calm and employs nonverbal cues such as relaxed, open, and symmetric posture, facial expressions, gestures, and a medium-pitched voice.

Aggressive Personality

An aggressive mode of communication is one in which the speaker uses a commanding and ineffective tone toward others. A dynamic person, in contrast to an assertive person, frequently uses a loud voice, glare, or scowling facial expressions; gestures are always fast and jerky, and they use postures that show they are superior to others. They are more defensive, intimidating, belligerent, demanding, and dangerous. These are negative influencers who frequently display pride and greed when in positions of authority. Aggressive communication usually makes the person on the receiving end feel threatened, humiliated, disrespected, and uncooperative in the conversation.

The Passive Style

Passive style is also known as passive-aggressive because people who use it appear normal on the outside but are bitter on the inside. People who use a passive communication style express their anger differently than those who use violence and aggression. That is, people who act in this manner are powerless and resentful, and as a result, they sabotage themselves. Communication behavior is typically untrustworthy, sarcastic, patronizing, and includes indirect aggression.

A soft and sweet voice, asymmetric postures, and a quick and jerky feature are among the nonverbal behaviors.

Style of Submission

Submissive people are those who seek to please others to avoid conflict, regardless of the difficulties they may face in the process. This communication style makes others feel more important and in control of a submissive person.

These people frequently exhibit apologetic, opting-out, inexpressive behavior, avoiding confrontations, and always feeling like a victim. Fidgeting and twisting gestures, soft voices, lack of eye contact, and still facing down and feeling small during confrontations are examples of nonverbal behaviors. People on the receiving end are frequently frustrated, advantageous, guilty, and irritated.

Manipulative Design

Though not necessarily the best communication style for everyone, manipulative people tend to become more cunning and cunning. This mode of communication has the potential to significantly influence others, particularly those who are feeling lost. When you try to push yourself up, these people become calculative and remain dominant in leadership positions. The language used usually conceals the intended meaning, leaving the receiving party unaware of the portrayed hidden meaning. As a result, manipulative people are more likely to become cunning, asking for things indirectly, sulking, controlling others, and making others feel guilty This communication style's voice is usually patronizing, ingratiating, and envious, with sad and pitiful expressions.

The Advantages of Understanding Communication Styles to Influence Others

Understanding the different types of communication styles puts you at the forefront of learning how to handle diverse groups under your leadership as an influencer who leads by example. Some people will use more than one mode of communication depending on the situation. As a result, understanding how they act and function in these situations allows you to deal with them effectively. You are free to use any style as a leader, but it must be respectful, reasonable, and beneficial to both yourself and the team or organization. Learning about different communication styles will enable you to be a good leader even in stressful situations in the future.

Specific Phrases and Words to Persuade Others

The English language contains five of the most persuasive words that have been discovered to influence people to engage in activities that influencers desire from them. However, other words are used in various fields, including business, to entice customers to buy a specific product. These words are used not only to persuade people but also to keep influencers in positions of leadership. Some of the most powerful words are: And 'And' is common conjunction used as a word to influence people, particularly when emphasizing specific information or products. For example, 'you have spent a significant amount of time reading this book, and there is still much to learn.' This means that no matter how far the reader has progressed and enjoyed the book, there is still more to discover. As a result, you are more likely to explore more than you expected if you continue reading. As you work to persuade people, the word 'and' encourages a reader to engage further, changing his or her decision, thoughts, and opinions.

This is yet another significant work that is used to provide additional explanations of what a given piece of information or product is all about.

The word 'because' has been used to create two distinct scenarios in a statement, indicating a better understanding of the receiving end. 'The grass is very green today because it rained last week,' for example. In this example, the word 'because' is used to provide context for the statement 'the grass is very green today.' As a result, this word attempts to provide an influential ability for an individual to comprehend the magnitude of a given event.

You

When you use 'you' to refer to life experience, you quickly separate your expertise from that of your reader or audience. Though some people use 'I' as an influential work, they both serve the same purpose. However, 'you' try to engage and communicate effectively, especially when influencing a larger audience. In some cases, using 'I' makes you feel proud and resentful of sharing your experiences with others. For example, 'as you read this, you will learn about different communication styles,' and 'as I read this, I will learn about different communication styles.' The first and second examples both emphasize the point. However, when it comes to persuading others, the first example outperforms the second.

Guarantee

To persuade people in the entrepreneurial sector, you must use more appealing and saleable language.

The term 'guarantee' is frequently used to describe product quality and durability. This is because the market is rife with fraud, and the only way to sell products is to make assurances to buyers. In this case, the term "guarantee" was used to persuade customers to buy a specific product based on the certainty of its authenticity. However, the business industry is full of other words used to persuade buyers, such as free, discounts, exclusive, and limited.

That is to say

The phrase 'which means' is also important for influencing people because it alters how they perceive specific thoughts and beliefs. Despite sounding like a common English phrase, it carries a powerful message that can influence the general public to engage in a completely new activity. Furthermore, depending on how you use them, they can be used as a comprehensive explanation of what specific action or attitude is all about. 'You've been in this class for a while, which means you're learning something useful for your life,' for example.

Persuasion and Influence Speaking Techniques

GETTING THE ATTENTION OF THE AUDIENCE

Influencers typically recognize the value of their audience and take advantage of the opportunity to engage with them by putting them first in the conversation. In this case, the technique entails considering your audience while ensuring that they are aware of and following your discussion. The first technique to use to influence your audience is to put them in the spotlight when highlighting your points.

That is, use the desired mode of communication to make your speech informative and exciting. Appealing to your audience increases the likelihood of them understanding and participating in the conversation.

Nonverbal Communication Techniques

Some people can deliver a well-organized, savvy, and plausible speech that leaves their audience satisfied with their subject matter.

Nonverbal cues, on the other hand, are more likely to keep your audience focused and excited during your presentation. Nonverbal elements include things like general appearance, emotions, gestures, and facial expressions. The use of both verbal and nonverbal elements not only drives the point home but also ensures that the speech is useful and delivered logically. At a glance, the combination of the two can significantly contribute to influencing more people.

Use of Practical Examples

Some topics require clarification due to their complexity or appear to be impossible. As a result, the audience may lose focus or perceive the presentation as focusing on an unattainable topic with limited considerations. In this case, the best way to make it more practical is to use actionable examples, preferably more than one. Furthermore, because they are the primary audience for your speech, you can use them as good examples.

Personal stories, experiments, and images displayed in the presentations are also acceptable examples.

Highlight Critical Cases

Even if you use both verbal and nonverbal elements, as well as relevant examples, some people may not stay focused and understand everything.

In this case, emphasizing key points in the statement is the best approach. The same effect can be achieved by pausing at every point where you believe the point is critical; using phrases such as 'listen closely' to emphasize the statements and changing tone and volume in these sections. You can also get closer to your audience and Maintain eye contact when emphasizing key points in your speech.

Engage the audience

To effectively influence people, it is critical to allow them to contribute to the topic at hand. Some people may remain silent throughout the speech without asking or adding to the question. In this case, you may fail to persuade them, particularly if you fail to engage them in the conversation. You can accomplish this by putting out a call to action, enticing them with plans, and preparing a closed meeting for them to share their thoughts on the speech. This technique has been used by several leaders who have engaged the audience and earned a good reputation. As a result, this technique allows you to gain the respect and trust of the people you want to influence.

CHAPTER 6

How to Connect with Anyone

Because we are connected to others, we will have different exposures and, as a result, different perceptions. However, unless there is an appraisal build-up, it is relatively difficult to connect with people we have recently met. It is beneficial to meet and hear different people's stories. The following are some pointers to help you connect with anyone.

Make the Best First Impression

When you meet someone, he or she will judge you based on your appearance. The first things the other person will notice about you are your grooming, approach, and behavior.

As a result, when you initiate a conversation with the individual, he or she will be attempting to justify their perception of how they saw you at first sight.

As a result, you should be impressive and decent to project a better image, even to people you've just met. When you decide to talk to or have dinner with the person, you should play your cards carefully.

To begin, you should use effective body language to demonstrate and portray who you should be. You should be conscious of your gestures, tone, and facial expressions. When leading the discussion, show enthusiasm, and compassion; how you say something is more important than what you say. Show an interest in learning more about and understanding the other person. As a result, you will build trust, which is the foundation of any productive relationship.

Start a Deep Conversation

We tend to make our conversations with people with whom we are not well acquainted to be superficial.

We only talk about what we see and, more broadly, what we perceive at the time. Learn to go beyond the surface level of conversation if you want to connect with more people. You should share your interests and preferences with the other person.

As a result, the other person will be willing to share his or her likes and preferences. However, you should avoid getting too personal, as this can lead to sensitive and unnecessary discussions.

Ask Clarification Questions

You should be interested not only in the other person's choices but also in the reasons for those choices. The decision could be about a career or a political stance. Demonstrate a desire to learn more while remaining objective. Eventually, you will understand the other person's point of view without making the conversation too personal.

Demonstrate Your Willingness to Learn from Them

Consider the person's social life when conducting your discussion. Demonstrate an eagerness to learn more from the person's story.

Similarly, do not project a dominant personality by dominating the conversation and presenting yourself as more experienced than the other person. You may, however, mention your area of expertise when necessary to demonstrate your abilities, but not to bluff.

As a result, you will form a bond with the person and instill a sense of importance in them. Similarly, the actor portrays a lack of pride as well as a willingness to learn from the other person.

Avoid Making Judgmental Statements

Your new acquaintance may reveal some personal or contentious decisions. By asking sarcastic questions, you must not make the person regret revealing his or her mask. Instead, express empathy and positive feelings about the other person's outlook on life. Equally important, if you disagree with their beliefs, you should first express empathy and then reciprocate by expressing your own.

Be Positive

There may be disagreements between your beliefs and those of the other person; however, this should not cause a schism. Recognize any positive aspect of the other person's story.

Cynicism tends to make the other person believe that you are hostile to his or her self-esteem.

Avoid frowning.

Make an effort to smile, as your body language can influence much of what you should say. A smile indicates that you care about the other person and are ready to mingle.

However, use a significant and relevant smile. It may appear awkward if you continue to smile even when the other person is delivering a painful encounter.

Personalize Your Discussion

At the first meeting, you should inquire about the other person's general profile. Throughout the discussion, use examples and statements that correspond to the person's status.

Similarly, when making an address, use the other person's full name. However, if the person has a title such as a doctor, professor, or honorable, make sure to include it with their name.

Create a Friendly Environment

The golden rule states that you should meet the expectations of the other person. You may hold opposing cultural views, but you are not required to criticize. Making the other person feel accommodated will lead to them opening up more, and as a result, you may end up creating intimacy.

Do Not Dispute

Remember that your meeting is not a debate in which you must prove that your point of view is correct. Contention will make the individual feel exhausted and believe you are attempting to lower his or her self-esteem Your viewpoint may be as good as, if not better than, that of the other person; while sticking to your guns will boost your ego, it will not help you connect with others. As a result, understanding the other person and using emotional intelligence to respond appropriately takes time.

Avoid Being Egocentric

If you want to connect with more people, you should silence your inner voice. Your ego may prevent you from connecting with others.

However, you should be genuine while avoiding exposing the schism between you and the new acquaintance. As a result, take the time to understand the other person without criticizing the issue that contradicts your stance; however, you can wisely present your point of view on specific topics.

Small Talk Can Help You Build Relationships

Small talks are conversations that you initiate to build rapport with a family member, colleague, or business associate. The guidelines below will help you approach the intended person and complete the small task.

Inquiry Concerning the Other Person

It could be your first meeting, or it could be with people you already know with whom you want to strengthen your bond.

Begin with General Questions.

Small talk exists solely to foster intimacy with the other person. As a result, regardless of how long you've known someone, you should be familiar with not only their appearance but also their perceptions, preferences, and likes. You can inquire about their occupation, residence, or activities. If it is a person, you may question how they perceive your behavior while also commenting on how you see theirs, their likes, why, and how they have made some decisions.

Ask More Specific Questions Later

You should ask more precise questions at this level.

For example, you could inquire about previous experiences or situations.

You can also inquire about their life goals and desires. You should, however, avoid making it appear overly sensitive.

Do Not Instigate Controversial Debate

There is a chance that you have different backgrounds or viewpoints. However, discussing an issue on which you have opposing views can make the other person feel uneasy. Instead, ask why they chose the positions, but don't linger on it. Differences in religion, political beliefs, or financial circumstances may exist.

When Asked to Respond, Use Clear Language

The use of ambiguous or colloquial language makes the other person feel uneasy, especially if they are unfamiliar with it.

Similarly, ambiguity can lead to incorrect interpretation. As a result, when answering the question and throughout the conversation, use complete sentences and clear language.

Creating Instant Relationships

Rapport in a relationship refers to mutual trust and respect. However, if you meet someone for the first time, chances are he or she does not know much about you. As a result, during the first meeting, you should exhibit characteristics that will establish an instant rapport. Here are some pointers on how to conduct yourself to establish an instant rapport.

Do not be concerned

You should feel at ease, act as if you've met the person before, and behave as you normally would. You should not fold your hands; instead, keep them by your sides. Hands folded may indicate that you are defending yourself due to uncertainty. Maintaining your hands by your sides, on the other hand, is a sign of openness and comfort.

Maintain Visual Contact

You should not shift your attention away from the other person. Look them in the eyes; this demonstrates confidence and interest. However, instead of staring at the person, look at them calmly. Looking at the person instills doubt and anxiety, making him or her uncomfortable. Maintaining eye contact, on the other hand, shows that you are confident and interested in what you are saying.

Refer to the Individual by Name

Knowing the person is the first step in developing a good rapport. Among the details, you should know the name; therefore, address the other person by name throughout the conversation.

Likewise, if the person has a title, it should always be attached to their name. For example, the person may be a doctor or professor; acknowledging the other person's accomplishment makes him or her feel honored, and they may be willing to form a relationship with you. However, failing to acknowledge this makes them feel unrecognized, which prevents you from establishing an instant and excellent rapport.

Make No Wrinkles on Your Face

Frowning expresses displeasure, sadness, or worry; how would the other person believe you if you addressed them while frowning? Frowning can also indicate anger and dominance. It can be interpreted that you believe the other person is of a lower caliber than you and does not require special treatment. As a result, talk with a smile on your face and enjoy what you're talking about.

A smile, on the other hand, is nonverbal communication, so use it wisely.

You should not bluff, nor should you alter your personality.

According to psychologists, the majority of lies are motivated by a person's dissatisfaction. A person believes that he or she is worth more than what they have. As a result, they shape their personalities to 'fit in' with the situation they believe they should be in. When meeting someone, you should be genuine and honest to establish an instant rapport. Similarly, do not use your accomplishments to intimidate the other person.

DEFINED HEALTHY RELATIONSHIPS

According to current research, many people are victims of unhealthy relationships. The latter, on the other hand, is revealed when the consequences are felt. A healthy relationship allows for equity and mutual equality. A healthy relationship is defined by communication and boundaries.

Communication refers to the exchange of information between partners. Communication allows the partners to gain a comprehensive understanding of one another. A healthy relationship has the following communication characteristics:

They are respectful and esteeming of one another.
They can all freely express their thoughts and feelings.
They demonstrate empathy for one another by understanding one another without prejudice.
They communicate with one another.
They do not assign blame.
They help each other achieve their goals.
They commemorate accomplishments and successes.

Boundaries are the limits that are set in terms of family, friends, persona; space, time, and sex life. In a healthy relationship, the participants exhibit the following characteristics in terms of boundaries:

The couple allows each other time with friends and family.

They do not keep track of each other's movements; instead, they trust one another.

They allow each other to do only what they are comfortable with.

RELATIONSHIP MANAGEMENT

You must maintain control over the relationship or it will destroy you. Here are some pointers on how to master your relationship:

Control over selection and connection: Relationships entail settling down with the people you chose; thus, you should learn the art of selection and connection.

Anticipate What You Want from the Relationship: Before you start dating, you should have a clear set of goals that you want to achieve through the relationship.

Follow Your Gut Feelings: When choosing a partner, you should go with your gut instinct. Your decisions should not be influenced by the appearance or convictions of the potential partner; instead, trust your instincts. Choose someone with whom you share basic perceptions and who will collaborate with you to achieve your goals.

Prioritize long-term goals over short-term situations: When setting goals, keep long-term achievements in mind. As a result, make decisions based on possibilities rather than the current situation.

Establish what is required for a Healthy Relationship: Any commitment comes with obligations, so you should focus on having a list of the institution's do's and don'ts.

Considering the requirements will assist you in selecting a partner who meets them as well as training yourself to do the one required on your end. As a result, you will have a healthier relationship with fewer dramas.

Settle with the Person Who Meets the Above Criteria: Because relationships are meant to last a long time, you should consider settling with someone who will help you grow.

Make it clear to your partner what you should and should not do in your relationship: The majority of relationships fail due to a lack of understanding. As a result, there are some things you must give up while incorporating others to have a healthy relationship.

Meet the Partner's Basic and Specific Needs to the Best of Your Ability: You should be concerned about your partner's needs. To avoid pressure and constraints while meeting the demands, you and your partner should agree on priorities.

Create an environment in which your partner feels at ease: Your partner may have some flaws. You should acknowledge and comprehend; do your best to find a loving and caring solution.

ADVANCED STRATEGIES FOR SOCIAL WEALTH

A social wealth fund is a limited amount of money and other public property. The wealth consists of shares and land that can be used for socially beneficial purposes.

Preparation in Advance

Plans are strategies that are put in place to be used in the pursuit of goals and objectives. An advanced approach, on the other hand, is the ability to leverage legal, regulatory, and financial resources.

Advanced planning will assist you in increasing and preserving your net worth.

The benefits of advanced planning are undeniable. Without a doubt, there are numerous ways in which the tax code and legal system can be legitimately capitalized to protect and, in some cases, increase personal wealth. Advanced planning is an effective method of structuring capital to avoid claims and provide legal protection from potential complainants:

Wealth Enhancement: This is the process of reducing taxes through advanced planning techniques, resulting in a more exceptional production of personal wealth. Numerous approaches can be used to increase income. For example, proper use of charitable trusts can be used to maximize wealth while allowing the wealthy to significantly support others. Private placement life insurance and flexible private placement installments are two options for people with a lot of money.

Estate planning is the act of legally organizing the eventual disposal of existing and anticipated property. Simple estate management techniques and financial products such as credit-shelter trusts or traditional life insurance are relatively simple and appropriate for many of the wealthy. For those with more complex situations, more advanced approaches such as self-canceling installment statements, grantor-preserved annuity trusts, and residual marital trusts for purchase are available.

Asset Protection Planning: This is the process of using risk management products and early planning strategies to ensure that an individual's or family's wealth is not tainted. Some approaches are overly simplistic and focus on dissociation. More refined asset protection planning approaches include transition strategies. In the right circumstances, the use of enslaved insurance companies can also be very effective.

Increasing Social Wealth

The total value of the services required to meet your psychological and social needs is referred to as social wealth. Social connection, on the other hand, is a form of social capital currency.

People with whom you regularly communicate, whether on internet platforms, face-to-face, or over the phone, are examples of social relations. This could include family members, co-workers, business associates, relatives, and friends. Each link has a unique value for you. As a result, each contributes separately to your estimate of total social capital. Close family members and close friends, for example, play an important role more than distant acquaintances Time also plays a role, so those with whom you interact more will participate more than those with whom you interact less.

Another aspect of social relationships is that they can be positive or negative. You may be willing to communicate with some people while refusing to communicate with others. People with whom you do not want to interact but are forced to communicate due to circumstances are an implication of social obligation. Net social capital is the sum of all positive connections minus all negative ties.

Social wealth is used to meet emotional needs such as safety, belonging, and networking. Because of social connections, being a part of a larger group allows you to feel much more prominent than when acting alone. Some of our biological systems have evolved to assist us in maintaining social communication since we are a social species. The satisfaction we feel from these systems gives us a sense of emotional well-being. The primary goal of social wealth is to provide two benefits:

Continue with the Psychological Needs: This is created through regular interactions with people. When you interact with people most of the time, especially those who are interesting to you and whom you like, you should feel emotionally well overall.

Give confidence in your ability to meet potential emotional needs. It has been established that the more social capital you have in times of emotional distress, the more confident you feel about meeting your emotional needs. It allows you to live more comfortably and improves the quality of your life.

CHAPTER 7

Developing Your Charisma

Charisma refers to the ability to attract, charm, and influence those around you. Charisma is viewed as a set of personal attributes and capabilities in aspects of leadership, such as the ability to project confidence, have an inner sense of purpose, engage others, and having the ability to articulate vision, ideas, and goals. Charismatic abilities, like any other, can be learned and developed. The intangible characteristics of charisma make it far more powerful than any other.

Charisma is derived from the Greek word Charis, which means "kindness and grace." It represented the qualities of beauty, charm, and creativity that humans possess. Regard, esteem, gratitude, elegance, and virtue are all components of grace. Executives, leaders, and divine creatures can all be defined using the oldest definition of charisma.

Historically, the word charisma was associated with supernatural elements. It was regarded as a gift from a supernatural being in heaven, bestowing the ability and authority to lead others. The modern definition of charisma includes self-assurance, charm, magnetism, personal ability, and the ability to rally others around a common goal or vision. People are considered charismatic when they are persuasive, which occurs most often when a larger vision is being promoted. Most leaders will act charismatically to attract the public's attention.

Grace is one of the most useful tools for understanding charisma.

Grace is an approach that has played an important role in redefining the role of charisma in leadership.

The term charisma is widely used in social sciences and religion, where it is defined and applied differently. Charisma, on the other hand, is a rare personality trait found in only a few people who can easily influence others. Charismatic people have a distinct sense of assertiveness dominance, calmness, authenticity, and dominance They also have exceptional communication skills.

CHARISMA CHARACTERISTICS

In many cases, you will encounter charismatic people but may be unaware of their true nature. Even in the face of adversity, great communicators will always capture their audience's attention.

These people are typically confident, optimistic, understanding, respectful, capable, genuine, and effective (C.O.U.R.A.G.E). Some people are born with a charismatic personality, while others learn it as they grow older. Some of the characteristics of charisma are listed below.

Confidence and charisma are inextricably linked traits. Confident people usually have a strong belief in themselves, which leads to others believing in them as well. Confident people have a distinct belief in their mental and physical abilities, which easily inspires others. These people always know what they want to bring to the audience and frequently associate with people who have strong network support and believe in them.

Charismatic people are upbeat and help others see opportunism as an important character in leadership. They always strive to persuade people to believe in them and see what they have to offer as beneficial to everyone. Goals set by charismatic people are realistic and intended to benefit everyone.

Charismatic people are known to listen more than they speak. Understanding and listening to others is something these people value. They are at ease making others feel appreciated and significant. They always speak only when necessary and spend the majority of their time actively listening to others.

Charismatic people are aware of their surroundings and their audience. They make every effort not to offend the ideas of other individuals Otherwise, they observe their surroundings and adjust their actions and boundaries accordingly.

Charismatic people understand their abilities as well as the abilities of those around them. By understanding this, they can set realistic goals that everyone in the group can achieve. They are aware of their capabilities and avoid situations that could lead to the failure of others.

Another characteristic of charismatic people is that they have good body language that matches their words. This allows them to easily persuade others to believe in them. Their body movements are natural as they speak, making them appear trustworthy and sincere.

Charismatic people are also effective. Their primary concern is providing a credible outcome. They want to help others succeed by delivering on their promises. They are always concerned with establishing a good reputation.

CHARISMA EVALUATION

Six common questions, according to scientific researchers, can be used to assess charisma. With these questions, you can calculate your score in terms of how charismatic you are. These questions include: I am someone who commands attention in a room, can influence others, knows how to lead a group, makes people feel at ease, frequently smiles at people, and can get along with anyone. Your charisma score is calculated by dividing your score by six and averaging the results. When your average score is higher than 3.7, you are considered more charismatic than the average person.

INCREASING YOUR CHARISMA

Charisma is not a genetic trait, but rather something that can be learned and maintained over time. Some people instantly make you feel important, while others simply walk into a room and add some charm. Some people are simply born with charisma. These individuals are capable of constructing and maintaining healthy relationships and always tending to make others think positively about themselves Everyone wants to be around people like this and aspires to be like them.

Being charismatic is unrelated to your level of success, how you present yourself, the image you project, or how you dress. This implies that everyone has the potential to become charismatic. What you do determines your charisma. These are the behaviors you exhibit toward others in your environment.

Developing charisma necessitates that you consider consistently following some guidelines that will assist you in achieving your desired goal. These are some of the methods for becoming more charismatic.

1. Listen more than you speak.

All it takes to demonstrate the importance to another person is to ask questions, maintain eye contact, frown, smile, nod, and respond nonverbally. When you listen to the other person, they get the impression that you genuinely care about them. Only speak up if you are asked for advice. When you speak a lot to offer advice, the conversation becomes about you rather than the other person.

Always speak only when you have something important to say or when it is relevant to what the other person is saying. This makes them realize that what they are saying is important.

2. Avoid Using Selective Hearing.

Always pay attention to what anyone is trying to tell you, no matter who they are or what level they are at. Always try to make everyone, regardless of social status or position, feel as if you have something in common. Do not pick and choose whom you will listen to and whom you will not listen to.

3. Clear Your Clutter Always

When you're talking to someone else, make sure your entire attention is on them. Avoid checking your phone or looking at your computer monitor frequently. Avoiding distractions from other things allows you to connect more easily with others. The gift of undivided attention makes others feel valued, and they will always want to be around you Most people will look up to you as a role model.

4. Always give before receiving, knowing that you may never receive.

Do not always consider how you can benefit from the actions of others.

Your focus should always be on what you can offer the other person and how you can assist them. Giving without expecting anything in return is one of the most effective strategies for developing and maintaining healthy relationships and connections with others. Focusing on what the other person can provide makes the relationship appear to be about you rather than the other person. As a result, to develop your charisma, always give without worrying about receiving it back in the future.

5. Avoid being too self-important.

Only people who are stuffy, self-important, and pretentious can benefit from your similarly self-important personality.

With such a personality, others will be put off, uncomfortable, and irritated whenever you are around them. People will frown if you walk into a room without first impressing them. It is critical to be humble and to treat everyone as an equal.

Developing charisma necessitates being authentically yourself.

6. You Should Understand That Other People Are More Important Than You

You are already conscious of yourself, your beliefs, points of view, and perspectives. You can't learn anything else from yourself because you already know everything. You are unaware of what other people around you are aware of, as well as their opinions, points of view, and perspectives. In most cases, not knowing more about other people elevates them above yourself. They are significant because there are numerous lessons to be learned from them.

Effectively connecting with and relating to these people will help you understand various aspects of life and what motivates them to act in certain ways. As a result, to develop a charismatic personality, always regard others as more important than yourself.

7. Make an effort to shine a light on others

Praise people whenever you tell them how well they did something. It is critical that you learn how other people performed and what they accomplished. Developing charisma necessitates showing appreciation for others whenever they win by making them feel you care about their activities. Appreciating other people's efforts makes them feel as if they have accomplished something and are significant.

8. Be Wary of Your Attitude and Your Words

The words people use to communicate have an impact on both their own and others' attitudes. Always strive to be fulfilled, enthusiastic, and happy to be more charismatic. When conversing with others, always consider taking a positive approach and using positive words. It gives you a sense of importance and makes you feel much better. Always make sure that your attitude does not put other people off, but rather that it lifts their spirits.

9. Avoid Discussing Other People's Failures

Everyone enjoys listening to gossip or dirt. The issue arises when people begin to dislike the person who is telling the dirt or gossip. Always try to keep other people's feelings in mind. Perhaps when someone tells you about what another person did, don't laugh at them because they might wonder if you do the same in their absence. Try to explain why they acted the way they did and how to avoid such traits in the future. Such ideas will portray you as a considerate individual who values other people's perspectives.

10. Be Prepared to Admit Your Fault

Nobody in this world is perfect, and we all make mistakes. It is not necessary to be completely charismatic to develop it everything is successful Always admit your mistakes and view them as lessons learned. When you laugh at your mistakes, the people around you will laugh with you rather than at you. People will always prefer to be around you because they like you more.

CHARISMA IN CONVERSATION

You may notice that the other person is not paying attention to you now and then during a conversation. This, of course, irritates you and turns you off. Being charismatic in conversations is essential because it gives the other person the impression that you are interested in what they have to say. Being fully engaged in a conversation may be difficult, but it is important to consider character development.

Practicing the tips will help you improve your conversational charisma.

Bring yourself back to the present moment. The process of being present in a conversation begins in the mind. In some cases, you may feel as if your mind is not settled and ready to begin the conversation. As a charismatic person, try focusing on someone's sensations, such as breathing or how your feet feel on the ground. Do this for a few seconds, and you will be able to return your attention to the connection moment.

Before engaging in a conversation, make sure you are physically comfortable. You can't be a charismatic conversationalist if you're preoccupied with how loose or tight your pants are. Always make sure you're comfortable and wearing clothes that fit you properly and make you look good.

Furthermore, getting enough sleep and consuming less or no caffeine can help to improve your physical comfort.

Consider switching your devices to silent mode or turning them off and keeping them away from you. You may notice that when you hold your phone, you are frequently tempted to check it, perhaps for social media updates, which gives the other person the impression that your attention is divided.

Putting your phone away reduces distractions and allows you to fully engage in the conversation.

Avoid fidgeting - This signal is thought to indicate that you are uneasy and that you are in the wrong place. Do not keep looking around while the other person is speaking. Looking around gives the impression to the other person that you are unhappy with your current situation and are looking for a better one.

Your entire attention should be on the current situation, and you should be actively listening to the other person.

When the other person is still talking, don't think about what you're going to say. When given the opportunity, almost everyone will jump in and start talking. Thinking about what \ you are going to give as a response is an indication that you are not \slistening to what they are saying. It is, however, critical that you consider carefully listening to the other person and thinking twice before responding. Do not feel obligated to fill in every silence period, but instead embrace any pause that occurs. It is always best to pause for a few seconds before responding. This shows the other person that you were fully engaged in their conversation and that you are taking your time to consider your response.

Advantages of Charismatic Leadership A charismatic leader has numerous advantages at work. Employees enjoy working with someone who has good communication and listening skills because of his personality. Charismatic leaders will always encourage their employees, even when they are facing difficulties.

Employee Support - Charismatic leaders can inspire and motivate their employees. They have a magnetic personality that allows them to connect with their employees well. Employees will always feel free to share their ideas and perspectives because they know their manager will take them into account.

Fun and an Improved Working Environment - When led by a charismatic leader, employees will always look forward to coming to work. This is because the leaders will make a decision.

A challenging work environment appears more appealing.

Charismatic leaders will always believe in their employees' potential, pushing them to achieve their full potential. This improves the working environment and thus increases employee productivity.

Setting a good example for other employees - charismatic leaders are frequently regarded as role models for their employees. Employees will try to emulate their managers' confidence, work attitude, and optimism. They eventually develop into potential leaders. The character they develop increases their chances of advancement.

Maximum Productivity - When led by a charismatic leader, employees will always strive to do their best. Absenteeism, poor attitudes, and poor work quality will be minimal. Employees believe they have a leader to whom they can look up and who cares about them. Employee turnover will not occur because employees remain loyal to the company and, even in a difficult situation, they trust their leader to help them get through it.

A learning process is prioritized by charismatic leadership. A charismatic leader recognizes that no one is perfect. They do not seek perfection in all activities in which their juniors participate. Such leaders will always provide their employees with the opportunity to learn from their mistakes. These leaders also draw lessons from their own mistakes. They see each mistake as an opportunity to make better decisions and avoid similar errors in future projects.

Charismatic leadership allows people to think differently about a variety of issues. Charismatic leaders are always open to sharing their vision and ideas with others. This gives people the opportunity to generate new ideas about a specific subject. People who are led by charismatic leaders are willing to take risks because they always provide them with a strong motivator. Being involved in a leader's ideas and visions gives people a sense of belonging, making them feel more important.

Charismatic leaders believe in the value of other people's ideas as well as their own. They can positively impact the lives of their juniors.

Being charismatic is a skill that we should all strive to learn and practice in our daily lives. This is because it assists us in developing healthy relationships with others and instilling a sense of importance in others. Charismatic individuals also contribute to social change. This is because we set a good example for those around us. We make them feel responsible for other people's presence by setting aside everything and giving them our full attention. Always keep the following important guidelines in mind as you strive to become a better person.

CHAPTER 8

How to Become Confident

Confidence does not come naturally; rather, it develops as a person grows. If you see someone with a lot of self-confidence, it's a good sign because the person has worked tirelessly on it for years Self-esteem is acquired rather than inherited.

Negative comments, business failures, and redundancies are some of the activities that can lower a victim's self-esteem. Even if they mean well, people can make you lose confidence with their comments.

There is also self-doubt, which is caused by believing you are unworthy of completing a task. The following are some of the necessary steps to help one become self-confident:

1. Make a Staff List

Making a staff list entail writing down things that one believes they are good at. This technique necessitates including every detail and not leaving anything out.

Are you an excellent storyteller? Are you a stickler for detail? Do you ever sing in the shower? All of these items must be included on the list.

Always go over the issues listed and be proud of yourself. Do not be afraid to show off your skills or list to co-workers and friends.

2. Understand the Art of Receiving Compliments

Accepting compliments shows maturity. The size of the tribute is unimportant, but where it comes from is. If it's a genuine compliment rather than one forced upon you. When complimented, thank the person.

There is no reason to refuse the compliment; instead, believe in yourself and be proud of it. The compliments boost your self-esteem. Do not mistake your colleagues' or friends' praise for sarcasm; instead, believe in yourself and own it. It may be difficult to accept after years of self-doubt, but with practice, one can gain control.

3. Instruction

Someone who reads a lot of books or considers himself/herself to be well-educated will be confident. Being aware of your surroundings, and underlying issues, and becoming acquainted with reading materials can all help to boost your confidence. It is not necessary to be an expert in that field, but having some knowledge about it can help. Learn about issues that are important to your colleagues and friends. This can be accomplished by reading about sports, politics, the economy, and fashion. Newspapers, sports, magazines, and current events are all sources of information.

4. Be open to new ideas and try something new.

Going on adventures and embracing new ideas can also help one gain confidence. What matters is the act of bringing your ideas to life. Taking risks in foreign lands, such as eating Chinese food, camping, attending a NASCAR race, and mountain climbing.

It's usually recommended that you try out new ideas at least twice a month. Don't give up easily, and if you don't like one adventure, try another one. With time, confidence grows.

5. Exercise and a Healthy Diet

There are numerous ways to maintain one's body without going to the gym. Some exercises, such as morning runs and swimming, can be done in the comfort of your own home or your neighborhood. A person can also seek the assistance of a trainer in the gym to assist. Eating healthy can also help someone's physical and mental health.

Consuming junk food daily can be detrimental to your health and even your self-esteem. Drinking plenty of water and switching from junk to healthy foods (fruits and vegetables) should be part of the routine. Healthy eating and exercise boost one's self-esteem and make one proud of one's accomplishments.

6. Change the People

You Surround Yourself with There are some people who always make you feel unworthy and voiceless, and bring a lot of negativities with them. Even if they are a close friend or relative, these are the people you must part ways with. Replace them with someone who sees your potential and encourages you. Someone who makes you feel good about yourself and does not make you feel used. Making new friends can be difficult, and leaving someone you've known for a long time can be even more difficult, but you owe it to yourself to try. These new people in your life can provide you with the necessary support to help you gain confidence over time.

7. Keep Yourself Amused by Dancing

When a person dances, the brain produces a chemical compound that aids in stress management. Going out to dance or even dancing at home to your favorite music. It doesn't matter where you are; what matters is that you have fun by dancing. Focus on yourself rather than what others are saying. You might surprise yourself; those around you will admire your personality.

8. Total Closet Makeover

Try on new clothes that are different from what you normally have in your closet. A change of clothing can be beneficial. Experiment with new outfits, jeans, suits, shirts, perfume, and deodorant. Shop with your friends and family members and allow them to assist you in selecting clothes that flatter you. You can still have a complete closet makeover while staying within your budget. Someone who looks good boosts his or her confidence.

9. Attempt to Do More Demanding Work

Many people find this technique strange, but it gradually builds one's confidence. Doing more work and completing assignments put one's ability to the test.

Carrying out these tasks allows you to meet new people within the organization

10. Learn to Recognize and Appreciate Others

This technique entails assisting those around you. Since you're working on your confidence, you've noticed that others are having the same issue. Act as a mentor to them and encourage them to improve their self-esteem. Take some time to thank your colleagues and family members for their assistance during your transition.

11. Adopt Positivity and Never Give Up

Don't give up when you're trying to accomplish something. Even if the going gets tough, do your best to stick with the activity.

Your desired outcome could be just around the corner.

There is a solution to every problem; it just depends on where you look. When you accomplish something, you experience a sensational feeling, which leads to an increase in confidence.

Reduced confidence can be caused by someone constantly thinking negatively and being told that he or she will fail. Still, think positively about your situation and whatever you want to do to stop this. Don't doubt your ability to complete the task at hand, even if it becomes more difficult along the way. Have faith in yourself and your worthiness. You are what you preach, and if you tell yourself, you aren't good enough, pretty, or strong enough to succeed, you will become those things. However, if you always think positively about yourself, your self-esteem will improve.

12. Be well-versed

Learn more about the tasks you've set for yourself, whether at work or home. When taking an exam, someone who is well prepared is more likely to pass due to their increased confidence than someone who is not well prepared.

13. Avoid comparing yourself to others.

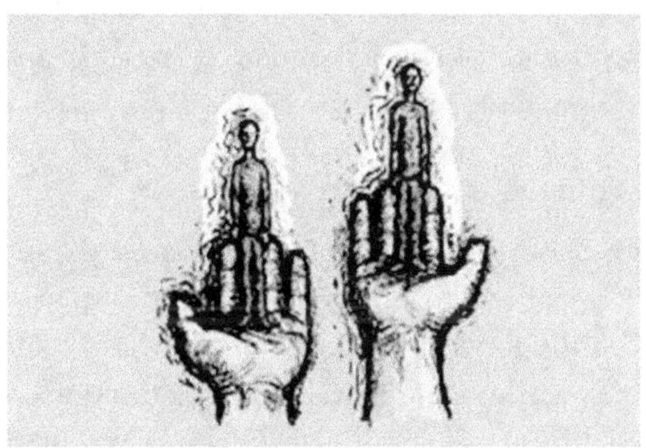

Comparing yourself to the accomplishments or personalities of others is rarely a good idea. It is not a good idea to compare your attractiveness, lifestyle, working environment, wealth, and job titles to those of your relatives, colleagues, and friends. It can cause depression and stress. It can also hurt one's self-esteem. In 2018, researchers discovered that people who envy others are more likely to have low self-esteem than those who do not envy others.

According to the studies, people who like to compare their lives to those of their friends are more likely to become envious, which leads to low self-esteem, and the more jealous he/she is, the more likely he/she is to become. When comparing your qualities, experience, and talents, keep in mind that you are doing more harm than good. Life isn't all about competition, and the sooner you realize that the sooner you'll be happy and content.

HOW TO DEAL WITH FEAR AND ANXIETY

Face Your Fears and Stop Avoiding Them

When fear takes over, you are more likely to stop doing things that make you happy or that you need to do. You avoid it because you are afraid of finding out for yourself.

Because of the fear, anxiety creeps in over time, which is not a good thing. To deal with this, you must take a stand and face your fears. Exposing yourself to it now and then can help you control it. You must face your fears, whether they are of snakes, a breakup, your parents, or losing weight.

Understand Yourself

Find out more about what's causing your anxiety and fear. Keep a journal in which you record things that happen during an event when anxiety strikes. Take some time to figure out what's causing the things you've written down in your journal. Set out to confront those items rather than avoid them. Make a list of the things you do to reduce your anxiety. The more you understand what causes your anxiety and fear, the better your chances of managing it are.

Exercising

Going to the gym or doing some exercises at home can help. It aids in the development of a strong mentality and mental focus, as well as the removal of fear and anxiety. Fear and anxiety are suppressed by the chemicals released by the brain during exercise sessions.

Relaxing

A relaxation technique can be extremely beneficial in dealing with fear and anxiety. The mind becomes at ease and mental strength increases during a relaxing period. It entails deeply inhaling and exhaling while moving the shoulder up and down. Another method for relaxing is to imagine yourself in a vacation destination, such as an island beach. When practiced, meditation and yoga can also produce positive results.

Healthy Food Consumption

This can be accomplished by replacing junk foods with fruits and vegetables. Reduced consumption of sugary substances and excessive coffee consumption Caffeine, which is produced by drinking coffee, has been shown to increase anxiety levels.

Reduce your consumption of alcoholic beverages.

Some people believe that drinking alcohol will help them solve their problems or manage their fears. Many people have been known to drink when they are stressed. Too much alcohol will not only not solve your anxiety problems, but will only make them worse. Courage does not come from drinking alcohol, but rather from conditioning your emotions to do so.

Spirituality and Religious Belief

Being spiritual allows others to connect to something they feel is missing in their lives. Following your religion's doctrines in times of stress and difficulty, and these lessons will help you cope.

Attending Therapy Sessions

One can choose to seek professional assistance by attending therapy sessions. When fear and anxiety have become major issues and you are unable to manage them on your own, therapy can help. Cognitive Behavioural Therapy, also known as CBT, can be used as a treatment modality. Several exercises are performed during the sessions to assist the individual in coping.

Medication

Medications can be used to help manage fear and anxiety, but they are known to suppress rather than cure them. It is not a sustainable solution. It is more of a band-aid solution that does not address the root causes of fear and anxiety. Drugs can be used in conjunction with other methods of fear management.

Groups of Support

There are people out there who have the same or similar problems as you do with fear and anxiety. Attending a group meeting with these people can be extremely beneficial.

Discussing fear with these people can provide you with more information on how to manage it, as some have already overcome it. The committee brings these people together to face their challenges together. The meeting includes stories, methods for dealing with fear, and words of encouragement from those who have overcome their fear and anxiety. Hearing stories from people like you provides an excellent feeling, and a connection is formed. Instead of those who are unaware of your situation.

Adopt A Positive Attitude

Learn more about how to maintain a positive attitude.

Think only of positive things because a negative mind breeds fear and anxiety. Do things that make you happy and bring you joy. Going to the beach with your family, watching comedy movies, and playing fun games with your friends.

The Importance of Self-Belief Brings Your Best Performance When Under Stress

Sportspeople, artists, and actors are examples of people whose jobs necessitate a high level of self-assurance. Those who lack faith are unlikely to succeed in this industry.

People perform better when they are confident.

Motivating Others

Those who exude confidence can inspire those around them to achieve more. Colleagues are likely to request help, and family members as well because you are an inspiration to them. Your working environment flourishes.

Improves Leadership Capabilities

Leaders are expected to be confident in their ability to address their people and complete their development projects. A great leader can motivate people to work together for the greater good. This can be accomplished by displaying self-assurance.

People will not follow someone who does not believe in himself/herself. Confidence and motivation bring the ability to lead. They must have faith in themselves and the projects they set out to complete for society.

Exuding a Lot of Positive Attitudes

Self-confidence gives one the belief to strive for greatness and to set higher goals. The courage to pursue higher-level goals and greatness.

The Appreciation and Respect Feeling

It inspires you to believe in yourself and to respect those around you. Because of your personality, friends and colleagues recognize you in the same way.

Being Attractive

Most people appreciate someone who is self-esteem is more appealing than a person with low self-esteem.

They prefer to be with someone who is a self-assured potential partner and are likely to find a partner appealing. A study was conducted that focused on relationships in both men and women. When dating, one looks for certain characteristics. Confidence was discovered to be the most desired quality among many of the participants.

Improves Positive Thoughts

It allows one to overcome self-doubt and set out to accomplish something he or she sets his or her mind to.

Fear and anxiety are reduced.

As they are comfortable in various sectors, confident individuals can take high-risk gambles in business that result in high returns.

Highly motivated and action-oriented

Having a high level of self-confidence allows one to be motivated to achieve his goals and visions. They are action-oriented and not only make plans but also take steps to make them a reality.

It inspires you to live your life for yourself.

The level of confidence can be used to define how others perceive you. People like confident people and will assign projects to them because they believe they know what they are doing. A lack of confidence can prevent you from achieving your objectives or goals. Anxiety and fear are a bad combination for success.

It communicates to others that you value yourself and others.

Individuals who lack confidence look to others to make them feel valued. There is no form to sign to be allowed to have fun and be happy. It is up to you to make yourself happy. Having a high level of confidence is more akin to having a positive attitude toward something.

When things get tough, you toughen up to face your challenges. Your efforts will enable you to complete the tasks at hand. Confidence is an important factor in making this a reality.

Positivity and self-assurance

Those who are always negative are difficult to associate with at work or home. People like being around those who have a negative personality and tend to avoid them. People who are more confident people optimistic than those who are less confident. They know what they are capable of, and if they set out to accomplish something, they will succeed. Those who lack confidence do not believe in themselves and prefer to discourage others with negative comments. They are fearful. When confronted with an obstacle, they do not attempt to solve it and instead stop, whereas confident individuals look for better ways to complete the task at hand.

Self-Belief Is a Sign of Maturity

Those who are self-assured believe in themselves and avoid people who try to bring them down with negative comments. They are not easily discouraged and have the freedom to participate in whatever they want.' The main indication during the puberty stage is a teenager's expectation, a proclivity for creative work, and a need for self-confidence building. The teenager unexpectedly exhibits signs of profundity in response to the impoliteness and embarrassment that he or she had previously experienced as a result of inactive indifference.

When you have a high level of confidence, it is much easier to engage in activities you enjoy. Those who can control their self-esteem and fear will find prosperity and success. When your workplace is toxic, you can engage in hobbies that will help you reduce your stress levels.

Fear and anxiety can be easily controlled if the techniques discussed above are used.

CHAPTER 9

Developing Communication Skills

Speaking abilities are the ability to communicate effectively to those who are listening. They enable you to convey a message in a more passionate passionately and convincingly ensuring that the audience does not misunderstand the speaker. Communication skills are abilities that can be used to give and receive information. Communication enables one to understand and be understood by others. Speaking, listening, and empathizing are all communication skills. When speaking, keep your thoughts straight; muddled thinking produces confusing messages.

Say what you mean, and say it with sincerity and truth.

Stay on topic and get to the meat of the speech.

Tell me what you want.

Be succinct - speak briefly and in familiar words.

Allow the true you to shine through for maximum clarity.

Be yourself, and you will be more at ease and convincing.

Make a mental image in your speech. A picture is worth a thousand words. When you stop, look, and listen, you have the best communication.

Tactfulness - Sensitive conversation always occurs at some point in the speech, and it is critical to approach such conversation n with tact when it occurs.

Emotional intelligence is essential during such a time.

Curiosity - asking questions to the audience demonstrates that you are interested in them — this is the best way to establish rapport with the audience. One of the most valuable skills in advancing your career because you will learn a lot and gain new skills Always be open to questions and keep the conversation going.

Friendliness - most people want to work with someone they feel at ease with. Being courteous and cordial goes a long way toward establishing a stable and reputable professional career.

Negotiation is a whole communication in and of itself, but it is still an important way of communicating. It is a useful skill to have when doing your job well. For example, negotiating a salary in an interview and negotiating a project deadline. Compromise and persuasion are important communication skills.

THE FOUR CS OF EFFECTIVE SPEAKING

Completeness - the message must be complete. Do not abandon your audience. The message is tailored to the audience's worldview.

Concreteness - a detailed message conveys seriousness in business conversations.

Courtesy demonstrates that you have a genuine attitude; it is more than just politeness with words like "please" and "thank you."

Correctness - correct verbal usage is preferred in business messages. Grammatical errors should be avoided at all costs. When oral is used correctly, it increases honesty and gives the audience the impression that the speaker is taking them seriously.

In communication, fuzzy language is prohibited.

Rather, clear language is distinguished by its explicitness, small sentences, and entire words. This gives the audience a clear picture of what you're saying.

Consideration - the speaker thinks about the audience to whom you want to convey the message. For effective communication, it is critical to relate to the target audience. When providing examples, consider the following factors: level of education, professional level, age, and audience interest.

Conciseness - when the storyline is consistent, the storyline is always clear. Even with the factors mentioned, it is still necessary to remain a constituent.

There are two more Cs to consider in communication that is often overlooked:

The use of sentence structure creatively will make the speech more enjoyable. When you use search terms creatively, you are being creative.

Credibility entails creating a trustworthy environment in a conversation. It is possible to achieve it with a bright and notable tone. It specifies that the information with which you are conversing is accurate.

ASPECTS OF EFFECTIVE PUBLIC SPEAKING

Effective speaking is the ability to say what you want, be heard, and have your message acted upon. There are some aspects of communication skills. They include the use of words, tonal variation in the voice, and nonverbal communication.

The words you use are extremely important. The listeners will return to the word you said to determine what you meant and what to consider.

The target audience - the words you use will vary depending on the listeners. In other words, the words you use with children will be different from the words you use to communicate with your colleagues. The words you use in front of 300 people at a conference will differ from the words you use in front of board members.

Short sentences are easy to understand and can convey sincerity.

Use simpler words- if you can't explain the words you've used, you probably don't understand the message.

The voice can reveal a lot about a person's emotional state. A person's voice can convey a lack of self-esteem. This means that someone with low self-esteem speaks in a low voice, whereas someone with confidence speaks in a commanding voice, resulting in clarity of the message. It is critical to become acquainted with and command your voice. It is possible to do so by recording your voice and carefully listening to it. Most people dislike the sound of their voices because is embarrassing.

The more you become accustomed to the sound of your voice, the easier it will be to hold a formal conversation. By recording and listening to the sound, you will become more familiar with your voice, making communication easier.

PRODUCTION OF VOCALS

Anyone who wants to be an active speaker must have these qualities.

Clarity - be comprehended to be heard,

Volume - Adding interest through a variety

Clarity: People like to talk while their teeth are clenched and their jaws are moving slightly, making them inaudible. To be able to articulate effectively, you must relax your jaw, expose your mouth, and give full benefits to all sounds you make. As a result, your listeners will be able to read your lips more easily.

It is also the rate at which people speak. When you speak too quickly, the recipients will not have time to confirm what you are saying. It's always a good idea to vary your speaking speed. Sometimes

You should quicken and then slow down to help keep your attention.

Volume: To create emphasis, you should sometimes raise the volume of your voice and sometimes lower the volume.

When you lower your voice to a whisper in the middle of a sentence, the audience becomes immediately aware. Always be cautious not to overuse the technique, as this will reduce its effectiveness.

When speaking in front of a crowd, try to convey the information with as much vocal energy and zeal as possible. This does not imply that you must speak freely. Make the speech as entertaining as possible. While speaking, emphasize certain words and expressions to convey meaning.

A pause is a prominent interruption in a speech. They can be used to highlight the effectiveness of the proceeding statement or to gain consideration before the critical report. Dramatic breaks convey a speaker's authority and confidence.

Voice preparation is always beneficial in any important speech. A speaker's voice is an essential tool. The length of your warm-up will be determined by how much speaking you need to do.

Language

Nonverbal communication accounts for the majority of communication.

Nonverbal communication includes pace, voice, and emphasis. Your body language, on the other hand, is just as important as your voice. Facial expressions, posture, hand movement, and eye contact are all examples of body language.

Real communication, as well as nonverbal messages, must be reinforced. Nonverbal communication is more effective ma ask rather than verbal If the speaker's body language does not convey the same message as their spoken message, it will be reflected in their opinions. You will need to think about how you want to use your body language, especially if you are trying to convey a difficult message.

When Speaking in Front of a Group, Always Pay Attention to These Signs

Blinking - If the audience is staring and blinking rapidly, it is a sign that the topic is boring or under consideration.

Those who avoid eye contact - This may indicate that the person has low self-esteem.

Rubbing one eye - When a speaker rubs one eye frequently, it indicates that the speaker is concerned about the response.

Feet - The audience stamping their feet after a statement indicates agreement. When a speaker stamps their feet, it usually indicates a lack of confidence in what they are saying.

Fingers - When a speaker rubs their forefinger and thumb together, it indicates that they are holding something back.

Smiles - Genuine smiles are common, and most facial expressions are fleeting. If a smile appears to be twisted, you may be looking at a fake.

HOW TO SHARPEN YOUR COMMUNICATION SKILLS

Make communication a right of way- this means that the message you are communicating should take precedence.

To improve your vocabulary, read books and magazine articles.

Keep it simple and to the point; this means using single words and straightforward language.

Engage your listeners- make the conversation enjoyable by asking questions and soliciting opinions. This will pique the interest of the listeners.

Take your time responding to a comment or question- After listening, take your time understanding and drafting your response.

Make certain that your message is understood by the audience. Don't blame the listener for not getting your point. You should rephrase and clarify the word so that everyone understands the message.

Develop your listening skills- If you want to improve your communication skills, you must first learn to listen. You should also avoid being distracted by what you want to say or respond to a comment. Always respond to a comment, never react to it.

Keep an eye on your body language- a larger portion of communication is nonverbal; this means that you should always be on the lookout for visual sighs from listeners, such as shaking, nodding the head, shaking the head, and visual sighs. Also, keep in mind that your body is sending the signal as well.

Maintaining eye contact- whether speaking to a group or one person, always maintain eye contact. You will demonstrate that you care about your listeners and that you are a credible person by doing so.

Understanding the message is not about you demonstrating that you genuinely care about your listeners. Genuine concern for the audience's needs will demonstrate respect. Another way to show respect is to listen to their responses.

An Exercise to Improve Speaking Ability

Find a book or a magazine, read the first two pages silently, then loudly in a normal talking voice, picking up and continuing until the end. Then reread it while recording your voice. Always keep in mind:

Relax- It is reasonable to finish the reading as soon as possible because it causes people to stumble over their words. When you are anxious, you read quickly, which makes it difficult to understand.

Keep your head up Try not to rest your chin on the book, as this will make your speech appear to be addressing the ground. Hold the book or magazine up and speak clearly.

Pause- Occasionally pausing at the end of a paragraph allows for a shorter rest and can be used for emphasis.

Always practice this, and you will improve.

The Importance of Breath in Speaking While Talking Voice is receptive to the excitement, it can occasionally become jammed, preventing the communication of various fillings.

As your muscles are in distress during a stressful situation, your breathing patterns will change. As a result, you can't use your lungs to their full potential. When you are scared, your neck and shoulders become tense. As a result, your voice is not being heard, making your speech difficult.

When using all of one's lung capacity, the breath will sustain the voice, making it more useful, complete, and resilient.

This will be useful for people who believe their voice is small and are concerned about speaking in front of a crowd. The tone of voice will be more orderly.

Breathing completely and to the beat is calming and therapeutic, releasing stiffness and promoting easing effects.

When you are at ease, you have more balance and are more receptive and assertive when speaking.

The Benefits of Speaking Ability

Excellent communication skills help to avoid confusion by providing clarity and a path.

Self-confidence is boosted by operational communication skills, such as making eye contact.

You'll be able to persuade people to agree with you once you've mastered the art of public speaking. This will give you confidence.

As clear organizational communication is very beneficial, the active speaker provides comprehensive and definite policies.

When you are an excellent speaker, you will be able to communicate goals in an organization, and as a result, employees will perform their tasks more efficiently.

Progression in one's career- When applying for a job or a promotion, you must demonstrate excellent communication skills. Communication skills are required here because you will be speaking with people from all walks of life.

When a good business is needed, proficiency in oral and written communication will come in handy.

Effective communication develops leadership skills; if you let others do your talking, you'll find it difficult to express yourself. You will not only be able to communicate fluently, but you will also be able to assist others. You'll change people's minds about something if you stand up and speak confidently.

Performance skills will benefit from effective communication. You will become more aware of when to speak and when to listen. Your articulation will become more precise, and you will gain confidence.

Profound communication enables you to speak concisely in a variety of situations to connect with others.

Effective communication strengthens relationships with customers. A customer's desire is to be understood by the corporation. Customers want to be heard and understood. This is useful when dealing with a large number of contacts.

The active speaker stands out from the rest of the crowd. You will be discussed based on how you distinguish yourself, not on your personality, but on how you communicate with others. Here are some personal benefits:

You have a natural ability to persuade others.

You can make your point without hesitation.

When necessary, you can negotiate more effectively.

You can better observe and analyze the situation.

Assist with the impact on interview situations.

The Importance of Effective Communication in Organizations; Sound judgment and problem-solving abilities

Production enhancements

Significantly convincing company resources

Workflow that is more powerful and well-organized

Strong business relationships

Writing as a means of communication

Writing skills are an excellent form of communication that aids in the use of data to provide examples, for example, when writing a business proposal to a company. Written communication should be formal.

Have an introduction and a conclusion that are brief and to the point. There is still a follow-up to complete the conversation.

It is critical to be able to converse effectively with listeners because it improves teamwork, inspires excellent performance, and promotes workplace values. Remember that communication is a two-way street. Always remember other people's nonverbal and verbal cues. If you learn how to speak effectively, you will be able to network in a more effective, constructive, and productive manner.

COMMUNICATION AND MANIPULATION

Manipulation is a type of social influence in psychology that focuses on changing the behaviors and perspectives of others through indirect tactics. Some methods of manipulating people are considered devious and exploitative when they serve the manipulator's interests. Manipulation, on the other hand, is not always cynical. It is sometimes harmless when the person being influenced is given the option of accepting or rejecting it.

Manipulation that works

According to George K. Simon, a famous psychologist, for manipulation to be considered successful, the manipulator must conceal aggressive behaviors and intentions, understand the psychological vulnerabilities of the person being manipulated to devise the most effective tactics, and can cause harm to the victim, when necessary, without fear of repercussions. In this case, a manipulative person creates a power imbalance to exploit a victim to further an agenda.

Why Do People Manipulate Others?

Almost everyone in today's world has been in a manipulative situation, and you're left wondering what drives the other person to behave in a certain way. Several factors contribute to Instead of being authentic, people use manipulative tactics to coerce others to do what they want.

Manipulation is motivated by feelings of inadequacy and fear.

People use manipulative tactics to accomplish their goals because they are afraid of not getting what they want.

They believe that manipulating others will help them achieve their goals. They are also afraid that the other person will succeed while they will fail. They believe that they should manipulate others to take advantage of limited resources. They also feel unworthy, so they do not have the best interests of others in mind. Manipulation occurs as a result of a lack of consciousness.

Many people fail to recognize that they are responsible for their reality, resulting in a lack of consciousness. These people are unconcerned about their global reputation. People who lack knowledge believe that being manipulative in the world is dangerous, but it is the only way they can succeed. They see manipulation as the only way to find happiness in life. As a result of manipulation, they feel emotionally and physically stable.

Manipulation's Effects

Most people use periodic manipulation as their primary form of manipulation. One example is when a spouse claims to be fine but is distressed. This type of manipulation influences the partner's perceptions and how they react to the spouse. Manipulation is frequently associated with emotional abuse, particularly in relationships. Many people will engage in manipulation because they believe they have the authority to control their surroundings, oblivious to the consequences.

Manipulation's Mental Health Effects - When left unaddressed, manipulation leads to poor mental health in those who are manipulated. The effects of manipulation are similar to the effects of trauma. This usually happens when the person being manipulated feels ashamed or guilty. People who are subjected to chronic manipulation tend to be depressed, develop unhealthy coping mechanisms, do everything in their power to please the manipulator, find it difficult to trust others, lie about their feelings, and frequently develop anxiety. People who are constantly manipulated tend to question their perceptions of reality.

Manipulation and Mental Health - Many people engage in manipulation regularly, which could be a sign of a mental health disorder. Manipulative people, in most cases, have personality disorders that lead them to believe that manipulation is the only way to meet their emotional needs. These individuals typically develop a coping mechanism in which they believe their needs can only be met by manipulating others. Others find it difficult to form healthy relationships with others, so they resort to manipulation as the only way to form a close relationship.

They use deception to keep their spouse or partner in the relationship. These people frequently shame, blame, and always exert control over situations.

Manipulation in Relationships - Long-term manipulative behavior often has an impact on close relationships. Relationships can be between family members, friends, or romantic partners. The health of the relationships formed deteriorates, resulting in negative effects on the mental health of those involved. Most relationships end or are dissolved because the people being manipulated feel they can no longer take it. The manipulated partner frequently feels worthless, isolated, and bullied. This is because their manipulators will always take control of any situation and dislike being questioned in any way. Some parents use manipulative techniques to raise their children. The likelihood of children using manipulative tactics as adults rises in such circumstances They became manipulative as a result of witnessing their parents' manipulation of them. and may believe that is the best way to raise children or deal with problems.

Friendships can also become toxic, and one partner frequently feels manipulated.

This is because one of their friends may be exerting subtle influence over them to achieve their objectives. Coercive tactics, such as requesting favors, are used by manipulative friends. They will only contact the other friend when they are in need, but will always make excuses when the friend requests a favor. They will also find ways to ask a friend to lend them money but will not repay it.

Detecting Manipulation

Manipulation is frequently classified into three types for ease of identification. One of the categories regards manipulation as a social influence that harms others. The second category regards manipulation as a form of pressure applied to others. The third category regards manipulation as a form of deception perpetrated on others.

Manipulation, as a social influence undermining other people, means that the manipulative person uses persuasion to influence the other person's behavior. The person being manipulated's capacities are bypassed, and their perceptions are influenced. It is trickery in the second approach to manipulation.

As a method of engaging in both philosophical and non-philosophical discussions about manipulating others. Manipulation is also regarded as a form of pressure applied to others. Peer pressure and emotional blackmail are two tactics used.

A person who is being manipulated is put under a lot of pressure because the costs of not doing what the manipulator wants are imposed on them.

CHAPTER 10

A Six-Step Plan for Making Your Dream a Reality

The world we live in will never be transformed unless dreams are transformed into actionable plans. Many people aspire to be prominent and successful, while others focus on doing something beneficial that will set them apart from the crowd. However, having a dream can become difficult when you fail to take the necessary steps to make it a reality. To accomplish this, you must first transform your dreams into goals, which will eventually become a reality. Dreams and goals are usually beneficial to us because they give rise to our life ambitions.

The Advantages of Having Dreams and Goals in Life

Motivation to engage in certain activities and reach one's full potential

Positive energy development is essential for overcoming obstacles while working toward specific life goals.

Dreams and goals keep you focused, preventing you from taking unnecessary steps and instead focusing on what is important.

They define who you are and what you want to become in the future.

Dreams add excitement to life while also providing possibilities for the future.

STEPS TO MAKING YOUR DREAMS A REALITY

Step 1: Imagine

Taking the first step in anything determines the result because it serves as the foundation for the entire process. That is, when you build a strong foundation, you are more likely to succeed, whereas weak beginnings usually fail. The same is true when it comes to making your dreams a reality. In this case, decide what you want to achieve by visualizing the final stages and how you will benefit. Some people may have multiple dreams but want to focus on the one that appears to be the most important. Create an endless supply of positive energy and engage in one that appears more attainable.

After deciding what you want to achieve, commit to it and get ready to embark on your journey to success. Most people may find this step difficult because making decisions can be difficult, especially when the dreams are sophisticated. That is, someone may have an idea for something unique but lack the necessary materials. Most of the time, they end up focusing on substitute dreams that were not their original idea.

However, it is critical to choose wisely and to reassure your subconscious that you will succeed despite the challenges that are likely to arise. After visualizing your desired dream that you want to meet, you are ready to proceed to the next step.

Step 2: Make a Strategy

Dreaming and having everything written down are two distinct things, which in this case is transforming what appeared to be impossible into something practical. The second step in making your dreams a reality is to plan out your strategy. Begin by highlighting your goals and breaking them down to meet the criteria provided. Furthermore, go into detail to learn more about your dreams, which usually allows you to see them as a reality. Getting organized and planning brings you closer to your goals and creates positive results energy, which motivates you to quickly engage in what is important in the process

The creation of a plan allows you to weigh multiple aspects of your idea, including advantages and associated disadvantages, as well as potential challenges. Some people may sit down and devise a plan that will return them to step one because the goals highlighted may appear difficult and unattainable, depending on their abilities. However, having a strategic plan accompanied by well-defined goals allows you to see your dreams in front of you. Though intimidating, each step you take brings you closer to realizing your dreams.

Step 3: Establish Networks

Nothing is more important than having a support system in place to help you achieve specific goals, especially if it is your first time. Most people who achieve their life goals seek the assistance of networks to guide them through the process. For example, if you want to start and grow a business, you could start by learning about the market through articles, consultants, or a friend. This gives you an idea of what you might encounter along the way. Building networks may not necessarily imply people, but rather other critical elements that would effectively drive your dream into reality. As a result, having a consistent support system is more likely to promote the achievement of your goals in the real world.

4th Step: Take Action

After you've put everything in place, it's time to pull the trigger and get started on the practical side of your dream. Develop your confidence by being inspired and focusing on what you want. Whatever decision you make, never be afraid to put it into action. These fantasies can range from going for a morning jog to taking out a large bank loan to buy a house. It is true.

Go for it, regardless of the scope of your dream or the goals that are driving you there, as long as you have a solid foundation.

Furthermore, once you commit to it and have everything in place, the signs will undoubtedly direct you to where you want to go and get what you want.

This is usually the most important stage of your goals, as you will now see what you imagined becoming a reality in the real world. To achieve an excellent manifestation of your goals, make certain that you follow your guidance, motivations, and inspirations to the letter. That is, never sway the moment you suspect something is wrong. Never be afraid to take on your first challenge. Continue forward while keeping the end goal in mind. You already have proof that the universe has accepted your dream, so go for it with both feet firmly planted. Furthermore, you will encounter more opportunities along the way if you work tirelessly to make your dreams a reality.

Evolving is the fifth step.

Everything we do produces results, which can be either positive or negative. However, if you follow the procedure correctly, you will have a successful outcome.

When you use an excellent guide to turn your dreams into reality, you are more likely to achieve your objectives. However, by being out there and taking steps in each process, you will discover numerous opportunities to grow and expand your knowledge. That is the accomplishments, manifestations, and experiences gained during the process change how you behave, allowing you to evolve in the market.

The experiences and knowledge gained throughout the process significantly change you, sharpening your techniques for achieving your goals. Everyone enjoys doing what they enjoy, and as you improve, you become prouder of what you do. While you're in your program, there may be some consequences that necessitate some changes. As a result, you can make any necessary changes or modify some of the approaches you used initially. You can keep evolving until you achieve your desired outcomes.

Step 6: Pursuing Your Dream

Nothing will make you happier than seeing yourself putting your dream to the test and reaping the benefits.

The primary goal of going through the entire program is often to transform aspirations into positive energy. Enjoy what you've only imagined while making the most of what's important. Regardless of your accomplishments, you must always maintain your focus. Furthermore, you can repeat these six steps with different dreams. That is, after making your first dream a reality, you can repeat the process with another vision, followed by others.

Some may choose to skip some steps because they are familiar with how to handle specific sections, but it is critical to remain familiar with these six steps.

OVERCOMING DIFFICULTIES AND SETBACKS

Dreams have long been regarded as valuable assets that must be safeguarded at all costs, and people should never lose faith in them. Pursuing our dreams is what keeps us going despite the difficulties we face daily. Even those who are successful continue to strive to achieve their goals and overcome obstacles.

However, there are methods for overcoming these obstacles and setbacks.

Make the Most of Your Network

When developing strategies for success and making your dreams a reality, you must create a support system that is beneficial to your process. To succeed in the process, you should surround yourself with a healthy support system, which may include friends, family, and colleagues, as well as some guiding elements. In this manner, you will receive the necessary advice and encouragement, as well as the necessary support, to achieve your goals.

Have a Solid Foundation

As previously stated, laying a solid foundation increases the likelihood of completing the process without major setbacks. Even if you decide to change your strategy in the future, having a well-established start-up ensures that you will rarely face challenges when attempting to change the foundation. Many successful dream chasers believe that it is critical to have a solid foundation that will not be shaken by waves of setbacks and obstacles along the way.

Adequate Preparation

Another important technique for dealing with setbacks and obstacles is mentally preparing for them because no one knows what the future holds. Create mitigation strategies for when they occur, both mentally and physically. Furthermore, ensure that your reactions have a limited impact on your goals, particularly in business, as this may cost more than the actual process. As a result, you will be at the forefront of avoiding impediments to your dream.

Maintain Concentration

This is one of the most effective methods for overcoming obstacles and setbacks because you focus solely on what you want despite the difficulties. Maintaining focus also allows you to quickly maintain your goals while avoiding situations that may have a significant impact on your motivations. When you lose focus, you are more likely to try to develop other goals to achieve your dream, causing more problems in the process.

Never, ever give up.

One of the hindrances to concentration is time, which is usually prolonged, resulting in impatience among individuals.

Another factor is a lack of self-motivation and confidence, which can have an impact on how you conduct yourself during the process. You should never give up in this situation because you are the only one who understands more concerning your aspirations Most people give up when they encounter a few roadblocks and setbacks due to a lack of patience, or when they face one or more challenges.

Learning Continually

Understanding what you are likely to encounter at the start and in the future is another critical technique for overcoming such obstacles. Consider reading various articles, videos, and books that highlight potential difficulties as well as notes from previous dream chasers. This gives you important insights into what is on the horizon. Furthermore, never stop learning because the world is constantly changing and you must keep up. As a result, there is more room to plan ahead of time for setbacks and obstacles that may derail your goals in the future.

How to Boost Productivity and Achieve Better Results

Have Faith in Yourself

When you believe you can succeed from the first step, you become motivated and increase your chances of success. For example, if you start on a high note and maintain it until the end, nothing, including setbacks and obstacles, can hold you back. When you internalize, agree, and commit to becoming a successful dream chaser, believing in yourself becomes second nature. As a result, you increase your chances of productivity and improve your results.

Have a Solid Foundation

As previously stated, having a strong foundation provides an unlimited opportunity to achieve more, especially for dream chasers. The first step largely determines the overall outcome of the process of making your dreams a reality. That is, once you have a completely standard foundation with adequate support from relevant people or elements, you are ready to move forward.

Maintain a Positive Attitude

Depending on how you engage with your goals, you may receive negative and sometimes critical feedback from various people. Some may embrace you, while others may act as roadblocks to influence you and affect how you proceed. In this case, the best way to avoid these 'haters' is to always be positive about what you do. Also, keep in mind that the future is what you hold on to, and if you base your decisions on the opinions of others, you are on the right track to hitting a brick wall.

Do Something Every Day

Making a plan to accomplish something positive every day is another way to boost your productivity and improve your results. When you start by creating a trend, you must accomplish something small, either small or large, and there is no doubt that you are increasing your productivity. For example, if you want to lose 70 pounds by jogging every day, start with shorter distances and then multiply by a few lengths daily. You can also incorporate some exercises after the jog, which provides an effort to achieve more than just jogging.

Share Your Objectives

Sharing your goals while lowering your expectations is another way to gradually increase your productivity. In other words, when you share your ideas, you may find some people who have more information on how to do it better or who will encourage you to keep going.

Sharing also allows you to broaden your knowledge because you will learn more from those who have already had a similar experience. In some cases, you may receive a better substitute for your goals, increasing your chances of success.

CONCLUSION

Thank you for reading Small Talk to the end; we hope it was informative and provided you with all of the tools you need to achieve your goals, whatever they may be. The next step is to get started and achieve what you've been hoping for a long time.

If you need to start a conversation with new people or make your friends feel safe when you don't have a topic to talk about, make small talk to help the interaction. There are numerous topics on which to base your conversation; choose one and practice your social interaction skills. Similarly, you may have dreams that are difficult to put on paper and make a reality. As a result, you will be provided with all of the necessary tools to make them a reality. Regardless of the difficulties that may arise, you are on the right track to making your dreams a reality.

Finally, if you found this book useful in any way, please leave a review on Amazon!